Creative Land Development

Creative Land Development

Bridge to the Future

Robert A. Lemire

Houghton Mifflin Company Boston 1979

Library of Congress Cataloging in Publication Data
Lemire, Robert.
  Creative land development.

  Bibliography: p.
  Includes index.
  1. Land use—Planning—United States. 2. Land use—Environmental aspects—United States. I. Title.
HD205 1979.L45   333.7'0973   79–17782
ISBN 0–395–28590–9

Printed in the United States of America

P 10 9 8 7 6 5 4 3 2 1

This book is dedicated to my wife and children—Ginny, Elise, and Bo—and to the people of Lincoln, Massachusetts. It is also dedicated to my parents and grandparents for their love and that of all our generations gone by. But, mostly, it is dedicated to all who care about the future.

"We abuse land because we regard it as a commodity belonging to us."

—ALDO LEOPOLD

"When we see land as a community to which we belong, we may begin to use it with love and respect."

—ALDO LEOPOLD

"So we need two million dwelling units per year in this country. Let's build them, but let's not destroy the countryside in the process."

—ROBERT A. LEMIRE, 1971

Acknowledgments

Although I am the author of this book, its substance is the product of the cumulative gifts of countless people. Major thanks go to the people of Lincoln for demonstrating that it is possible to blend development with the protection of natural resources in building a balanced community. But the Lincoln story is one of community achievement. It is impossible to single out any of the countless town officers, landowners, and citizens who helped me see that we are limited only by our vision and determination. The same is true of the countless individuals in communities, agencies, and organizations throughout the country who have shared their experiences. I can only hope that this book does sufficient justice to what we have learned so that others may add to the process.

My greatest thanks go to my editor, Ruth Hapgood, who had the courage to commit herself to this book when it was just a dream and for her skillful guidance in helping me make it a reality.

I am grateful to Margaret P. Flint for generously providing the book's diagrams, to my wife Virginia for typing the early manuscripts, and to Jacquelyn Snelling for typing the final text.

Many individuals helped me a great deal during the year it took to research and write the book. I especially want to thank David Morine of The Nature Conservancy, John Clark of The

Conservation Foundation, and Robert Allen of the Kendall Foundation for their encouragement and suggestions. I am also grateful to the following for valuable interviews and contributions: Darwyn Briggs of the USDA Soil Conservation Service; Tom Mierzwa and Toby Pierce of the EPA; Justin Blackwelder, Peter Huessy, and Wilson Pritchett III of the Environmental Fund; William K. Reilly, president of the Conservation Foundation; and James Howell, chief economist for the First National Bank of Boston. I am also grateful to the many staff respondents at the nine regional planning agencies who provided the reports and observations that made my quick tour of the sites of the country's resource conflicts possible. To the many others who helped but have not been named, my sincere thanks.

Foreword

By the time the environmental revolution surfaced on Earth Day 1970, I had been active for seven years in the long and intense efforts of the people of Lincoln, Massachusetts, to deal with Metropolitan Boston growth pressures that threatened our town's rural character. Nevertheless, it wasn't until the environmental awakening of the 1970s that I began to see the relevance of Lincoln's efforts to the nation at large. By then we had come to recognize that the threat we feared was not inherently one of population growth. We had come to understand the fast-changing economics of holding large parcels of undeveloped land that were forcing these parcels into house lots. We understood that the threat to Lincoln's physical character was really a threat to its open fields, wetlands, tree-shaded roads, and the network of trails that traversed both public and private land.

By the mid-1970s Lincoln's success in guiding and shaping its growth while protecting its rural aspect had generated a great deal of publicity and outside interest. It also resulted in my being drawn into the land use activities of other communities, regional associations, and state and federal agencies. Out of all this has come an unexpected view of what's happening on the land use scene in the United States. It is a general view, a citizen's view, and not the professional view of a specialist or the self-interested view of any sector of our economy or government. As such, I hope that it makes up in balance what it may lack in expertise.

Contents

Acknowledgments   ix
Foreword   xi

CHAPTER ONE
Growth and Land Use in the United States   1

CHAPTER TWO
America's Threatened Land and Water Resources   12

CHAPTER THREE
Growth and Land Use Conflicts in the United States   29

CHAPTER FOUR
Land Conversion in Lincoln, Massachusetts   55

CHAPTER FIVE
Outreach, Teaching, and Consulting   112

CHAPTER SIX
The Creative Process   145

Notes   157
Bibliography   159
Index   163

Creative Land Development

CHAPTER ONE

Growth and Land Use in the United States

THIS BOOK IS about an explosion—the rapidly changing use of land in the United States—and what we must do to achieve a balanced relation with nature. Our country has more than two billion acres of land. Cities, towns, highways, shopping centers, and places to live, work, and play eat up more and more land —the same land that is needed to support our rapidly growing population. As this population grows from 220 million to more than 300 million over the next twenty to thirty years, we must create new relations between man and his environment, because the old ways cannot provide what we need—neither now nor in the future. I am writing about the demographics, resource economics, politics, laws, and attitudes behind the decisions that shape our national land use patterns and about the ways that communities, small groups—even individuals—can become involved in the land conversion process to make it life enhancing rather than destructive.

Most of us are not aware that our landscape is the product of our cumulative land conversion decisions. Freed from the land, or at least under the impression that we have been freed from the land, most of us are not aware of the unsustainable demands we have begun to place on the land; we take land and its gifts for granted. We have lost the ability to distinguish between the diverse forms of land, and we convert it indiscriminately from one use to another to meet short-term needs. Having turned from the soil, most of us fail to see the signs that cry out for a more careful treatment of the very source of our being. In my search for a new land use rationale, I have been particularly moved by a handful of broad indicators of the urgency of these problems. We will soon be forced to care about the way we convert land in the United States.

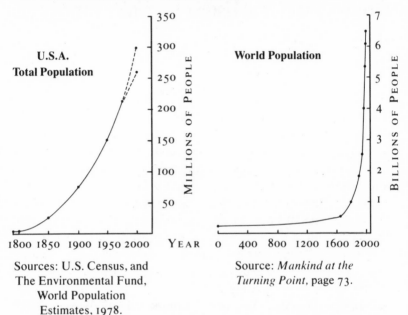

Sources: U.S. Census, and
The Environmental Fund,
    World Population
    Estimates, 1978.

Source: *Mankind at the
Turning Point*, page 73.

Population growth is at the root of our demands on the land. More people need more housing, more work and play space, more food, more water, in short, more of everything that requires land for production or for space. Land and natural resources are limited, our world is limited, and it is clear that the sharply rising population trends will be limited as well and may even collapse. The question is not if, it is when. The planet is hard pressed to support 4.3 billion people. In twenty years it will be called on to support an additional 2 billion, or 50 percent more. Our own country struggles to maintain living standards for 220 million. How will it fare with an additional 80 million, or 35 percent? All the while, nonrenewable resources are being consumed and dispersed at a growing rate, leaving less for the recovery that one hopes will follow the collapse. As indicated in the following population chart, the higher the peak, the lower the base that will follow.

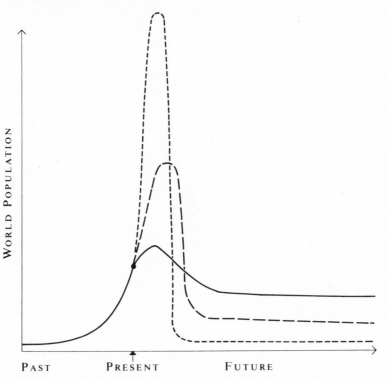

Adapted from: *The Consequences of Delay*, Wilson Pritchett III, The Environmental Fund, November 1978.

One clue to the timing of the population peak is provided in the following diagram by M. King Hubbert, the elder statesman of American oil geologists.

Many believe the industrial and technological revolutions made possible by the discovery of fossil fuels sustained the geometric population explosion that began in the early 1800s.

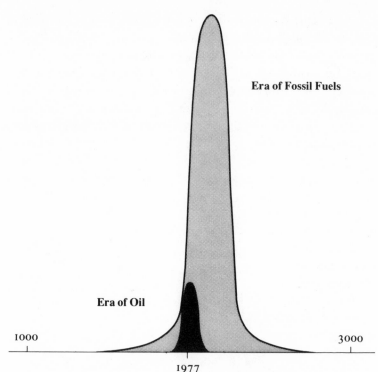

Era of Fossil Fuels

Era of Oil

1000

3000

1977

Source: "When We'll Start Running Out of Oil," Peter Nulty,
Fortune, October 1977, pages 246 and 247.

It's easy to overlook the fact that petroleum has become an essential ingredient of, or contributor to, everything we eat, wear, or use. As we near the crossover point where oil consumption must decline in the face of reduced availability, how can we project continued population growth when the more likely prospect is collapse? How will we deal with decreasing fuel for our tractors, trucks, and planes? What will we use to replace our petroleum-based fertilizers, herbicides, and pesticides? Will we turn to our farm fields to produce gasahol in competition with food? Will we have to grow more cotton, wool, and hemp to meet the decline in synthetic fibers? Will coal and other substitutes fill the void? If so, at what cost?

Equally serious for the human prospect is the limited availability of potential farmland on a national and worldwide basis, the slowdown and possible reversal of the long improvement curves in farm yields begun in the nineteenth century, and the rapid loss of fertility on present farmlands. As if that weren't enough, we now learn that the whole population explosion was incubated in a temporary period of abnormally favorable world climate which already shows signs of having begun to regress.

These are the essential facts of life that nobody really wants to move onto the national and international agendas. These are the facts that should have primary consideration in the planning of our settlement patterns. And yet, as we move into this age of scarcity, our land use patterns are geared to an age of plenty. Having allowed our cities to sprawl in the great technological and population surge that followed World War II, we perceive the solutions to our most urgent land use problems largely in terms of what the federal government can do to solve them. At present this turns out to involve massive aid to our debt-ridden cities at the expense of our energy-hungry suburbs and impoverished rural areas; the protection of millions of acres of wilderness while little is done to save millions of acres of needed cropland from irretrievable conversion; and the building of huge dams and water management systems to satisfy avoidable competing needs temporarily. As we battle over these issues, the ways by which settlement patterns can be balanced with long-term food, water, and energy resources have yet to be defined. And our national strategies fail to take into account the local decision-making nature of our land conversion process.

Abundance of fossil fuels and related machinery in our worldwide technological society allowed our population to swell from one billion people in 1830 to 4.3 billion in 1978. Demographic dynamics are driving toward a world population of 6.5 billion by the turn of the century. We are confronted with an absolute decline in the availability of petroleum and natural gas well before that time. Adequate dependable alternate sources of energy to support the expected population growth cannot be projected beyond the immediate future.

The postpetroleum age into which the United States is moving is very different from that of the past thirty years. Most of the world's potential farmland is already in production. At best an additional 10 percent increase in productive farmland can be expected while the world population grows by 50 percent between now and the year 2000. Preparing for an age in which the world population may have to retreat toward preindustrial numbers is simply not being considered. But if we will not act as a nation, we can and must act as individuals. In our local communities we can begin to identify and protect renewable resources, to reverse our growing dependence on distant sources for vital resources. Only then can we regain our independence and begin an orderly shift toward a healthy equilibrium within our limited life support systems.

Communities all over the world can no longer afford to plan their development in expectation of an ever-increasing supply from other areas. Having set the pace toward indiscriminate land use, America must awaken to its rapidly changing global context and provide guidance to its states and municipalities. The options to do so exist, but they must be perceived.

The job of building and rebuilding the United States never ceases. It didn't end with the massive construction required to accommodate the 80 million increase in U.S. population realized between 1940 and 1975, nor will it end with making room for an expected 80 million more Americans and illegal aliens between now and the year 2000.

In conducting research for this book I have become aware of a growing national concern over the disturbing rate at which productive farmland is being lost. I have found it reassuring to learn that federal steps have begun to identify and catalog our prime and unique farmland. In late 1978 both the Environmental Protection Agency (EPA) and the U.S. Department of Agriculture set forth policies to minimize the loss of farmland through federal action. These new policy statements reaffirm the rights and responsibilities of state and local governments to develop public policies and to plan and regulate private land use. State and local initiatives will be required to protect specific pieces. Let us proceed therefore with the clear understanding that saving our vital natural resources is largely a matter of private stewardship along with state and local government responsibility.

In the course of my research I have also come to realize that the financial stakes in protecting our essential natural resources can be more than we as a society can afford. The U.S. appetite for land is such that more resource land is threatened with development over the next twenty years than we can afford to lose. We seem to be confronted with two major choices to stop the loss. The first is to zone land into its permanent resource use without compensation—a forced capital levy on the landowners involved. Although challenged in the courts and at the ballot box, Oregon has succeeded in protecting most of its 2 million acres of prime farmland in this fashion. The other approach is to compensate landowners by the public purchase of so-called development rights. Several states and counties have already started this approach. Both approaches entail substantial risk. In a showdown the courts may require compensation which, for whatever reason, may be more than we can afford. To purchase development rights of America's 400 million acres of cropland alone would cost more than $1 trillion.[1] To avoid this financial bind, we must have more creative approaches to saving farm and other vital resource land.

Many argue that there is no problem, that free market conditions will result in optimum land use patterns. It is obvious that farmland will stay in food and fiber production if food and fiber prices are sufficiently high to support higher values per acre than those offered by developers. But what happens to food prices when markets have to capitalize land prices at $4,000 or more per acre instead of $400? Doing nothing, then, means that we as a society will have to pay for farmland's development potential in the form of higher food prices. If that's the case, we might just as well face up to the problem once and for all and buy development rights. Having fought for them in Massachusetts, I am well aware that development-rights programs are proposed to combat higher prices, but I do not believe such programs should do the whole job.

Are we without choice then? Must we either deny our farm owners and other owners of land of public interest the right to realize a higher value for their land or trust the courts and voters to protect needed resources? Must we spend trillions to save these resources? Or, worse yet, must we suffer still further losses until food supplies decline and food prices soar beyond the reach of many of our people? Fortunately the answer is no. The United States need not founder on this apparent dilemma. Population growth and change need not eat further into the natural resource base we all will need. Regulatory powers can be safely applied to save resource land that is too fragile or not safe for development into competing uses. Moreover, it is possible to save resource land and have appropriate development too. Careful review of state and federal programs for roads and sewers can guide growth away from vital resource land to areas where it will be welcome. Sharper definition both of the land resources to be protected and of human growth needs to be satisfied in each community can lead to compatible development that serves to protect rather than conflict with needed resources. Public land acquisition and other tax-related protective approaches can then be focused on those parcels where other alternatives do not exist. Land values can be more precisely determined to assure fair value to both public and private interests. The key lies in a clearer understanding and articulation of the options available to each individual landowner when the time comes to convert his or her land from one use to another. But first we must understand the perceptions and processes that have brought forth our present condition. Next we must identify and catalog our resource lands of public interest and determine their ownership and conversion prospects. Where conflicts with their future resource values are identified we must resolve the conflicts in favor of resource protection while dealing fairly with owner interests. Once equity interests have been fairly acknowledged there is no reason why local officials should not be allowed to move on to their charge of building healthy, balanced communities.

To date most of our resource protection has focused on the need to shelter resource land from the path of population growth and changing land use preferences. Much land has been saved from development to meet owner interests without full consideration of public interest. More has been protected in large chunks without real consideration of possible compatible development. The tendency has been to consider that threatened parcels will either be totally protected or totally developed. There has been little effort to penetrate the ownership veil to distinguish portions that could or should be developed and those that should be protected. As a result land saving has been more a political than a rational process. Where it has become rational is largely in the protection of such fragile or unsafe areas as wetlands or steep slopes. Here constitutional police powers have been used to regulate development. As the need to save buildable resource land has become apparent, there has been a tendency to stretch the police powers to prohibit unwanted development. Although the courts have gone a long way toward supporting this Old Testament "thou shalt not" approach, there is good reason to fear that this approach will not protect all the resources that require protection. At some point the whole constitutional issue of what constitutes a taking under the Fifth Amendment could blow up into a serious compensation problem. Even if this issue is contained, there is the whole matter of adequate equity consideration. How long can we deny farmers the "right" to sell their land into development to realize higher than farm values?

Public purchase at fair market value has been the other major approach to protecting valued resource land. We have reached the point where annual federal spending for land acquisition exceeds $1 billion. Ignoring whether we are purchasing the right or the wrong land or paying too much for what is bought, there remain such awesome questions as: What happens if we continue to purchase land at the present rate for twenty years only to find that while we were saving parks and selected wilderness areas we had lost 40 to 50 million acres of needed cropland and our populations had swelled from 220 million to over 300 million? What happens if declining petroleum availability diminishes our chemical-intensive agricultural production, our food processing and delivery efficiencies? What happens if changing climatic conditions seriously reduce food production, already concentrated in a few areas? These questions suggest a real land use agenda that must be addressed. Perhaps we should be applying some of our public land acquisition dollars to the task of defining our real land use problems and the options available to us.

In Lincoln, Massachusetts, and elsewhere, we have learned to protect natural resources while stimulating needed development. I know that our American communities have many more land use options than are commonly perceived. I have seen wetlands saved through mapping and appropriate zoning and regulation. I have seen farmland and aquifers protected both by outright purchase and by zoning options that enabled owners to realize the full dollar value of their land through the careful development of those portions suited to development. I have learned to appreciate the possibility of saving valuable resource land through the building of concentrated subsidized housing as part of an effort to achieve multiple public goals at minimum public cost.

What has been learned in Lincoln has been carried elsewhere and successfully applied. My land use experiences in Lincoln and elsewhere have led me to numerous communities in several states and have involved me in our state's efforts to deal with its loss of farmland and its water supply and wastewater management programs. What has been learned has been documented, studied, and ordered into a teaching curriculum so that it may become a tool for application elsewhere. It is the subject of this book—an attempt to set forth the major population and land use facts of life that confront our nation, to show the inadequacy of our major federal and state land use initiatives, and to suggest the broad national relevance of the lessons we have learned while building a balanced community.

CHAPTER TWO

America's Threatened Land and Water Resources

GLOBAL AND AMERICAN population numbers and behavior have reached the point where our natural support systems can no longer be taken for granted. Faced with another doubling of the global population over the next thirty-five years, we must take stock of our natural resources and guide growth to minimize conflicts with the vital resources we will all require. If our tomorrows are to be better than our yesterdays, we must establish an equilibrium between people and earth's natural support capabilities. Nowhere is this more important than in the United States where our frontier heritage and technological perspective have led us to use up land as though it were a limitless commodity instead of a community to which we all belong.

A look at the earth's land resources, and our own as a part of that base, should awaken us to the need to deal with the land kindly, to recognize that all land is not the same, to be careful in choosing land to convert from such vital life support functions as food production and water supply, and to work purposefully at the task of providing suitable land for housing, work, and recreation.

To achieve this we must become acquainted with America's resource base and learn to distinguish between land that needs protection and land that can be developed wisely to satisfy different human needs. Then we must become adept at resolving potential use conflicts through effective planning, incentives, and regulation. In essence, we must learn to harness the vitality of growth and change to building socially balanced communities—communities in which natural systems are protected at minimum public cost yet with full respect for the equity interests of present owners. Clearly this will require considerable change in the way we go about converting land in the United States.

The earth's total land area is 33.8 billion acres; maximum arable land is estimated at 5.9 billion acres. Of this, 3.5 billion acres are in cultivation cycles with 2.3 billion acres harvested each year.[1] At first glance there are ample land reserves to produce food for the growing world population. Yet we know that three-fourths of the world's 4.3 billion people are inadequately fed. Is this because owners of potential farmland are obstinately keeping it out of food production? Or are we really reaching the limits of the globe's food production capabilities?

We know that most of the unfarmed arable land is covered by tropical rain forests in the Amazon basin of Brazil and the Congo region in central Africa. Slash and burn operations in Brazil have already exposed 10 percent of the Amazon region to tillage. Many are deeply concerned about the global ecological repercussions from exposing these fragile tropical soils to erosion and desertification. The harsh facts are that most of the world's farmable land is already under intense cultivation and that 20 percent of it is expected to lose its fertility to erosion and poor farming practices in the next ten to twenty years. It is in this context that we must consider America's finite land and water resources.

As recently as 1974 the U.S. Department of Agriculture (USDA) published a fact-filled booklet entitled "Our Land and Water Resources, Current and Prospective Supplies and Uses." The main theme of this publication echoes the traditional sense that the United States is rich in abundant natural resources, that food and the energy required to produce food will never run out, that in fact our basic resource problems are ones of surplus management. This view was implicit in the following first paragraph of the publication's introduction signed by then USDA Secretary Earl Butz:

Although thousands of acres of farmland are converted annually to other uses—and population has risen a third in 20 years, we are in no danger of running out of farmland. Increasingly efficient production methods, a declining rate of population growth, and an abundance of water resources and land with agricultural potential should ensure our domestic food and fiber needs to the year 2000 and leave enough land left over for other purposes.[2]

The report divides America's land base of 2.3 billion acres into two broad categories of agricultural and nonagricultural land. In 1969 agricultural lands totaled 1.3 billion acres, or close to 57 percent of our total land mass. Of these 333 million acres, or 15 percent, were used as cropland, with an additional 51 million acres of cropland idle or in soil improvement crops. Of the balance which was in grassland pasture, range, grazed forest land, farmsteads, and roads, 88 million acres were considered suitable for use as cropland. By deduction, there was a ready cropland reserve of 139 million acres implying a possible 40 percent increase in crop production. Moreover, looking to the year 2000, the report projected a need for only 272 million acres of cropland providing an expanding reserve buffer as time passed. Nonagricultural land in 1969 was categorized as 525 million acres in forest land not grazed, 61 million acres in urban use including roads and other built-up areas, 81 million acres in recreation, park, and wildlife use, 27 million acres under public installations and facilities, and 28 million acres in miscellaneous uses including such areas of little agricultural use as marshes, bare rock areas, deserts, and tundra.

Since it had taken close to 350 years to convert 61 million acres into all our urban and related uses, since the report projected an increase of only 20 million additional acres in these uses by the year 2000, and since no real change was seen to be taking place in the balance of America's resource base, the 1974

USDA publication on our nation's land and water resources raised little public concern.

Even as the 1974 report was being written, however, rapidly changing world circumstances raised serious questions about U.S. agricultural policies and the management of our natural resource base. First of all, world demand for U.S. food soared between 1972 and 1975. Despite suspension of the old cropland "set-aside" programs to curb production, surpluses disappeared as food became an export offset for foreign oil imports. At the same time the annual pattern in yields per acre became less predictable than during the previous two decades, when steady growth in yields was the norm. From 1950 through 1969, thanks to favorable weather and widespread application of new agricultural technology, the United States had experienced a steady increase in food production despite a decrease of over 50 million acres in cropped farmland. By 1972 total U.S. crop production was 149 percent of the 1950 level and yields per acre had reached an all time high of 167 percent of the 1950 base levels.[3]

This changed in the early 1970s, when we were hit with soaring world demand, less favorable weather patterns, changes in petroleum availability, a break in the steady trend toward better yields, and escalating food prices. Suddenly agriculture became a broad public concern and not simply a political matter involving food producers. But this was soon forgotten as in the mid-1970s favorable weather patterns returned, foreign demand slackened, and cropland reserves were back in production. By 1978 it looked like a return of the old problems of abundance with a return of federal "set-aside" programs. Like the gasoline station lines of 1974, the specter of world hunger was soon forgotten, but not by all.

A 1975 USDA soil conservation study of cropland availability published in 1977 revealed that ready cropland reserves were nowhere near the 200 million acres believed to exist in 1969. The 1975 study showed a cropland base of 400 million acres with only an additional 35 million acres readily available for tillage.

Another 76 million acres identified as having high or medium potential for conversion to cropland were seen to face significant conversion problems that would require additional expense and effort to convert them to cropland. These problems include high-density forest cover, seasonal high water table, and high erosion hazard. Moreover, 24 million of these 76 million acres were deemed to be earmarked for development into urban and other build-up uses. Still the nation appeared to have a healthy cropland base of 435 million acres. This 1975 report also noted that between 1967 and 1975 forest land declined from 445 million to 375 million acres while pastureland and rangeland increased from 507 to 571 million acres and land in other farm uses increased from 57 to 70 million acres. Clearly there was a lot of land use change going on in the United States that was not covered by the simple prevailing notion that we have been losing a net of 1.2 million acres of farmland per year and that everything else has been staying pretty much the same.

What amazes me is the sense of complacency that continues to prevail in our high government offices. Despite the fact that by 1978 the Land Use Executive Committee of the USDA was aware that farmers were cropping 367 million acres and edging toward the upper limits of the 385 million acres then considered to be readily available for use, the committee did not see a "major crisis" brewing. In a draft policy statement dated October 1978, this committee acknowledged the growing pressure on America's cropland base and yet expressed its belief that America's cropland base would hold up under the stress of the added food demand and competing uses. It noted that the loss of 2.5 million crop acres per year was partially offset by the addition of 1.3 million crop acres per year to the nation's cropland base through expanded irrigation, drainage, land clearing, and development of dryland farming. It did not note the decreasing availability of potential replacement cropland or the cost of making it tillable. Nor did it deal with the ecological costs of land clearing and dryland farming. The draft report did stress the need for care, calling for well-considered policies concerning farmland use and conservation. It noted potentially important future constraints on production including higher energy costs; restricted water availability with depletion of groundwater stocks; unfavorable weather; increased costs of nonland inputs; environmental restrictions; a declining rate of advancement in agricultural technology; continued conversion of productive farmland to nonagricultural uses, and volatile export demands. Yet in spite of all this the committee stated that the situation was not a "major crisis." I suspect that their choice of language was political. Clearly a crisis is advancing upon us, particularly in view of the observation by Lester R. Brown, director of Worldwatch Institute, that at least 30 percent of our cropland is suffering net topsoil losses every year and can be expected to lose much, if not all, of its fertility over the next twenty years.

Nor does the 1978 draft policy statement of the USDA Land Use Executive Committee fail to recognize our looming farmland shortage as a national and world hunger situation. The politics of the situation are such that they write of it as a state and local land use issue only. They identify their role as offering research, educational, technical, and financial assistance to states and local communities interested in protecting farmland in their jurisdictions. To their credit, like the Environmental Protection Agency (EPA), the USDA has implemented review procedures to minimize the loss of farmland to federally sponsored projects. But at the American Land Forum's first conference, held in Washington, D.C., on December 20, 1978, which dealt with issues of farmland retention in the United States, I was startled to hear Norman A. Berg, chairman of the USDA Land Use Executive Committee, say that he could not point to a single acre of farmland that had ever been saved by the USDA. I had the feeling that he was lamenting the limited role that the USDA can play in actually saving American farmland. This should change soon. In the meantime, I hope this book will help states and local communities protect some of the vital resource land we will otherwise lose.

In addition to the obvious loss of cropland to other uses, other factors are combining to make the protection of our remaining base even more acute. The gradual destruction of much of our cropland through our modern high-energy-, high-petroleum-based agricultural practices has been amply documented by Wendell Berry in *The Unsettling of America.* We are just now becoming aware of the effects of air pollution on crop yields. Charles E. Little of the American Land Forum has written that studies undertaken in Southern California have shown that polluted air caused declines in yields of 38 percent for alfalfa, 32 percent for black-eyed peas, 32 percent for lettuce, 72 percent for sweet corn, and 38 percent for radishes.[4]

Similar experiments in Massachusetts have demonstrated declines of 15 percent for alfalfa and sweet corn, 25 percent for beans, and 33 percent for tomatoes. These losses are not confined to industrial and urban areas. Agronomist Joseph P. Biniek has found that pollutants travel hundreds, even thousands, of miles through the atmosphere, undergoing added chemical changes to finally fall out as deposits of dry particulates or acid rain. It is so easy to forget how fragile nature's reproductive processes are.

There is the further concern of climatologists like Neil Bryson who forecast planetary cooling trends that could seriously alter weather patterns that have been favoring food production in the breadbaskets of the world. Surer restraints on our expected pattern of high yields per acre include eventual shortages of key fertilizers such as phosphate and the disappearance of cheap energy.

While there may be little we can do about some of the problems confronting American agriculture, we certainly don't have to continue converting good farmland, particularly cropland, away from food production. If we fail to do this, how will we feed America's population in the year 2000 and beyond? Or how will we respond to the demands of developing countries projected to need 50 to 85 million tons of grain imports by 1985, let alone thereafter? Again the question must be asked: Is the loss of U.S. farmland strictly a matter for state and local concern?

Having reported on the crises confronting our nation's land resources, I am almost reluctant to reveal the comparable state of our water resources. Here again we have a basic and limited resource whose quality and abundance have too long been taken for granted. We have uncoordinated use and fragmented government control, leading to the management of symptoms instead of the overall system. Our fractured approaches to dealing with this essential resource have turned the abundance of rain that falls onto our land into polluted and scarce supplies. Worse than that, we have converted our abundant water resources into conveyors of so-called wastes that otherwise would be recycled to sustain future generations.

Average precipitation on our nation's forty-eight conterminous states amounts to 30 inches per year, or 4,200 billion gallons of water per day. As a natural system, this abundant precipitation falls on the land and drains into watersheds and river basins. Some collects in mountain pools, lakes, and ponds while some pauses in swamps and marshes and as groundwater in our porous subsurface soils. Through absorption, evaporation, wind, and rain, this cycle continues through the years and is available to nourish life and serve its many needs. Of this precipitation, some 70 percent is transpired directly back into the air by vegetation. Roughly 40 percent of this is a natural loss while the other 60 percent provides the moisture for 80 percent of our supply of food and fiber and nearly all of our forest products. The remaining 30 percent, equivalent to 1.2 trillion gallons per day for the forty-eight lower states, is natural runoff and can be considered the effective renewable supply. This is augmented by accumulated groundwater. These reserves, not all of which can be economically tapped, are equal to about thirty years of runoff.

Sadly, our failure to understand and accept our nation's hydrologic cycle in all of its complexity has resulted in excessive competitive use in certain areas, the needless fouling of needed surface and groundwater supplies, and the poisoning of our ultimate water purifier, the atmosphere. Despite enormous expenditures, our water resources and their control and delivery systems are still being abused. It should, therefore, come as no surprise that water supply has joined food and energy as a future crisis issue.

As California has recently learned, most of our land use patterns presume an inexhaustible supply of cheap water and are dependent on the favorable weather patterns of the 1950s and 1960s. Simply put, we live in a society where development is allowed to take place without due allowance for the vagaries of weather and other contingencies. As a result, for example, we find ourselves facing monumental conflicts in the West between some 30 million acres of irrigated farmland, coal and oil shale development interests, and the needs of rapidly growing urban areas. In the short run, of course, problems can be postponed by mining groundwater. But in many areas of our country the short run is either behind us or our groundwater has been polluted. This was revealed in a late 1978 discussion paper published by the EPA, which noted that the water-short areas of our country are also those which depend most strongly on groundwater for supplies. Indeed, some regions are seriously depleting this resource by mining. "Groundwater depletion is widespread in the Texas-Gulf, Rio Grande, Arkansas-White-Red, Lower Colorado, and California regions, plus portions of the Upper and Lower Mississippi and the South Atlantic Gulf regions. Continuation of mining could ultimately exhaust local supplies and create severe shortages."[5]

Although it is late in the game, water supply, water consumption, and wastewater management must be coordinated and made part of our growth management process.

This will not be easy because of the long-standing legal and political context in which water usage decisions are made. As in the case of agriculture, water issues are essentially land use issues and constitutionally fall within the jurisdiction of states and local governments. The problem is further complicated by our two systems of water rights—the Riparian Doctrine, which governs water use in states east of the Mississippi, and the Appropriative Doctrine, which applies in states west of the Mississippi. Both serve to protect vested interests which are often in conflict with the systemic interests of our nation's hydrologic cycle.

As in the case of farmland, there is a growing awareness at our federal level that the nation must take a holistic approach to the management of its water resources. After spending over $200 million under Public Law 92–500 to plan for wastewater management, the EPA in a recent water supply and wastewater treatment coordination study calls for a rethinking of our fractured approach to these two important water issues.[6] At last we seem to be moving in the right direction.

Nevertheless we are still prisoners of our past development practices. Some in the West eye Alaska's water resources as a solution to their problems. Representing the largest block of undeveloped water supply in the United States, Alaska's natural runoff is about 580 billion gallons per day, or almost half that of the entire lower forty-eight states. Such a diversion raises some interesting issues, not the least of which are the dollar and energy costs required to deliver the water.

Even in water-rich Massachusetts we are considering diversion of the Connecticut River to meet the water needs of the highly urbanized eastern part of the state. As a citizen adviser to this proposed diversion, I can assure you that diversions are complex ecological, social, and economic issues. Whether or not this diversion takes place, we in eastern Massachusetts now know that water prices are going up, that water is no longer essentially a free commodity. This is what happens when we approach water problems community by community. Only now is the Commonwealth of Massachusetts in the process of adopting a comprehensive water supply policy.

My main point is that U.S. water resources are limited, that we have already begun to exceed those limits, and that further population growth and possible climatic changes will make water supply a critical future issue. As we plan to accommodate growth, we must take the complete water cycle into consideration. For example, we must anticipate water conflicts between urban, industrial, and agricultural uses. The future water shortages we face raise important questions regarding the wisdom of our policy of planting houses on naturally watered farmland and replacing it with irrigated land. Unfortunately, there's no cheap turning back in this game of land conversion.

There's no cheap turning back because resource land is usually lost to development or earmarked for development while the resource activity, often farming, is allowed to decline in anticipation of that expected development. This process takes place largely on the fringes of our urban communities, which may spread fifty miles and cast a development shadow on all the enclosed farmland. In 1970, 139 million people, or about 70 percent of the U.S. population in the lower forty-eight states, lived within 242 metropolitan areas on 13 percent of the land mass of these states. Between 1960 and 1970 these 242 metropolitan areas had gained 19.7 million people, or 83 percent of the net increase of 24 million people that took place in these states.

The importance of this growth conflict with food production is masked by the statistic that only 14 percent of U.S. harvested cropland is located in these same areas. Vegetable and fruit farms have historically girdled our population centers. Even now some 60 percent of our vegetables and 43 percent of our fruits and nuts are grown in our standard metropolitan statistical areas. Development pressure on this farmland is particularly disturbing in light of nutritionist Jean Mayer's observation that fruits and vegetables are our main source of minerals and vitamins and that Americans are already consuming only a fraction as much of these products as Europeans. In other words, our most threatened farmland produces some of our most needed nutriments while our least threatened farmland is used to produce bulk grains that can be readily stored and shipped. As a result U.S. agriculture is increasingly geared to foreign trade and decreasingly suited to meeting the real nutritional needs and taste satisfactions of our people.

The loss of productive farmlands in such heavily populated areas as the Northeast is also an emerging economic concern. I was pleasantly surprised, for example, to find in an interview with Dr. James Howell, chief economist for the First National Bank of Boston, that he now sees the need to protect local agriculture as an import substitute after having believed that it had no long-range economic justification in an urbanizing state. Such a change in attitude in the business community could be of great importance in planning to halt the loss of farmland near population centers.

But the development and implementation of such programs is not going to be easy. First of all, land conversion is largely a matter of ownership and America's land and water resources are broadly held by owners who are very jealous of their "property rights."

Only thirteen of our fifty states require comprehensive planning or zoning, and approximately three-fourths of the private land in the United States is without any zoning or planning whatever, giving individual owners broad leeway in determining the future use of their land. It's not the absence of zoning and planning as effective tools for protecting needed resources that bothers me. Experience shows that these have not worked to protect farmland in populated areas where zoning and planning have prevailed. What really bothers me is the thought of millions of landowners making conversion decisions without consideration of their cumulative effects on our overall resource base. In some way the common good must become a part of these decisions.

Nevertheless, I have strong reservations against forced land use. But that doesn't mean we shouldn't find out why land is being converted the way it is and explore ways to relieve the pressures that may be forcing unwanted decisions or create incentives that help foster beneficial decisions. In short I believe that enlightened self-interest can and must be harnessed to the creation of balanced settlement patterns that are in harmony with our natural systems.

But for enlightened self-interest to work there must be enlightenment, and that means general awareness of what's going on. Although about two-fifths of the land area of the United States is government-owned, the balance is held by 60 million others. According to Dr. Gene Wunderlich, an economist with the USDA's Economic Research Service, America's 26.3 million acres in residential use have some 50 million owners. Another 40 million acres of private land classified as commercial, industrial, nonfarm, waste, and miscellaneous are owned by about 3 million entities. Taken together, land conversion decisions of these owners would seem to have little direct bearing on our agricultural future, although they could have considerable influence on our housing and job future. To the extent that these owners make decisions that absorb or fail to absorb much of America's future growth, they could have a significant secondary influence on the future of our farm and forest resources.

Of greater farmland and woodland significance are the 7.5 million owners of the 1.2 billion acres of our range, farm, and forest land. Included were some 2.7 million farms in 1969 of which 151,000, or only 5.5 percent, accounted for 54.5 percent of America's farmland. Clearly what these 7.5 million owners and their successors decide to do with their land will largely determine the future of our land and water resources. After all, they control 95 percent of our nation's nongovernment-owned land. Since the cumulative effect of their decisions could have serious implications for our resource future, it would seem to be a good idea to develop a detailed understanding of the pressures that will influence their decisions. Several of these will be looked at in later chapters. The principal root of most of these pressures, of course, is population growth.

Although there is considerable controversy about the extent of population growth over the next twenty to forty years, there is little doubt that large increases will occur. Some, like Senator

Daniel Patrick Moynihan, are comforted by the expectation that global population will grow by only 28 percent to 5.5 billion by the year 2000 instead of the 51 percent growth to 6.5 to 7 billion projected just a few years ago.[7] These now project global stability at 8 billion in 2010 or 2015 instead of 10 to 13 billion around the year 2030. In contrast the Environmental Fund, which concentrates on global statistics, vehemently maintains a global projection of 6.5 billion for the year 2000. Given the pressures already exerted on the earth's resources, that extra billion people by the year 2000 could pose an impossible burden.

Similarly the 1975 U.S. Census Bureau projects likely U.S. population growth of 19 percent, or 40 million, to a level of 260 million by the year 2000 and further continuing growth to 290 million by the year 2020. The Environmental Fund, on the other hand, projects U.S. population for the year 2000 at 305 million. Much of the difference is attributed to projected illegal immigration. Despite these contradictions, demography has much to say about the future. I wonder, however, to what extent demographic projections take into account our rapidly changing resource base. I find it difficult, for example, to project an easy doubling of earth's population or 38 percent increase of the U.S. population over the next thirty-five years. Matching any of these projections with my earlier numbers on available farmland alone leads me to the conclusion that we must begin a systematic study of our resources with all the diligence we have given in the past to waging wars, conquering disease, or placing a man on the moon. Moreover, forgetting for the moment the probable peaking of available petroleum in the 1980s and the widening geographic separation of population from its vital supplies, it strikes me that we must judge the adequacy of our food-producing capability and policies in terms of world needs at prices people can afford.

In this context I mourn the millions of acres of cropland already lost near our American cities and elsewhere, and I worry about the small reserves that we treat so lightly because we do not as a society recognize their importance or their relevance to our individual lives. How many people know how much food can be grown on an acre of farmland or how much land it takes to grow a person? These are questions that most of our grandparents or great-grandparents could answer because they lived on the land that fed them. It is precisely this kind of illiteracy that allows the gradual erosion of a whole state's agricultural base without effective public response.

Early in 1976 I was called on to prepare a paper on the economics of saving the remaining farmland in Massachusetts.[8] Having extracted acreage data on a county-by-county basis from a comparative land use survey based on 1951 and 1971 aerial photographs,[9] I struggled to find a rationale for saving our last 700,000 acres of farmland, including 300,000 acres of cropland. The commonwealth's 5.8 million people eat $3 billion of food annually, of which only $200 million is produced in the state. Why bother then to spend $150 million or more dollars to protect land that would support only 400,000 or so people when more land was needed for houses and industry? It was then that I learned what an acre of cropland can really produce. In my home town of Lincoln we are growing 12,000 ears of sweet corn per acre. That's a lot of food. In reading Helen and Scott Nearing's *Living the Good Life* I learned that they had succeeded in feeding six people by gardening one-third of an acre in Vermont with minimum equipment and almost no artificial fertilizers. That's when I realized that the remaining farmland in Massachusetts had to be saved. After all, it had the potential of feeding the Massachusetts population in a crunch, particularly if its use were carefully managed along with backyard gardens, brooks, ponds, and the ocean.

In other words, if Massachusetts were to become a fully industrialized state, it would lose all hope of a possible self-sustaining future and become fully dependent on distant sources for the sustenance of its population. Looking ahead to an age of energy scarcity, this argument alone would have supported the need to save our rapidly dwindling farmland.

Fortunately, my economic analysis showed that savings in transportation costs and protection of tax revenues from our agricultural community more than justified the proposed public investment. More about this later.

Since writing that paper I have learned from John Todd of The New Alchemy and others that energy, fertilizer, and dollar-efficient food production need not be a land intensive process. I have eaten delicious lettuce and tomatoes grown on water—carriers immersed in a 2,000-square-foot warehouse by Lee Frankl of Cape Cod. In all instances, however, the principals have argued for the protection of farmland to meet today's needs and those of tomorrow. Although it is comforting to know that there are pioneers in agritechnology working on techniques that may free much of the globe's farmland to other uses, any conversion to technological agriculture will be slow and expensive and may be filled with false starts. In the meantime, prudence requires that we prepare to meet the needs of the next twenty to fifty years with the resources at hand.

Although this is not intended as a book on farmland, I find myself particularly concerned with the protection of this resource. To date much of our spending on resource protection has been oriented to wilderness areas, parks, and recreation areas. I am all in favor of protecting these important resources. All the approaches to guiding growth and change in this book should apply.

If I am particularly concerned with farmland, it is because there seems to be a particular crisis brewing and too little is being done to deal with it. I am pleased to see leading environmental organizations such as The Nature Conservancy, the American Land Forum, the Sierra Club, the Conservation Foundation, the Audubon Societies, the Trust for Public Land, the National Trust for Historic Preservation, and others begin to focus on farmland retention as a major land use issue. After all, if we were to ask ourselves how valuable are our acres of threatened farmland, we'd have to answer that they are as valuable as the lives they can support.

In an age of food scarcity we either have to bring that land back into food production or the people will die who would otherwise be dependent on the farmland. A classical economist would argue that the general price levels of food will be driven to the marginal cost of bringing into production the last few acres of farmland needed to produce the minimum level of required food. Clearly, at today's land costs, we as a free society cannot allow ourselves to be driven to these circumstances. Fortunately there is an emerging perception that agriculture is a vital component of a healthy regional economic mix. This is a point of view that can help rally the public and private sectors of our economy to effective farmland protection policies and practices. To the extent that some of our threatened valuable farmland and other valuable resource land lies in the path of urban sprawl—so-called buckshot development—or other patterns of growth, we must learn to work our way around it in ways we can all afford. As will be demonstrated in subsequent chapters, there are many ways to do this without imposing unfair burdens or penalties on the owners of these important lands.

As I see it, protection of our water resources will be more a matter of integrating our water supply and wastewater management programs into our overall land use planning and implementation. To the extent that growth must be guided away from special water resources, the same growth-guiding techniques described for saving farmland will be shown to apply.

CHAPTER THREE

Growth and Land Use Conflicts in the United States

IT'S GOING TO take a lot of new houses, work places, and public facilities to accommodate a 40 to 85 million increase in our population by the year 2000. Although there are shifting patterns of regional population growth in America along with an easing of the long migration from rural to urban areas, it is expected that the bulk of our growth will settle in and around existing metropolitan areas. Nevertheless, assuming a continuation of present trends in lifestyles and personal goals, a substantial part of this new growth and settlement shifts will generate severe development pressures in rural and remote areas. Add to this the additional population growth expected between the years 2000 and 2020, and the result will be the conversion of a great deal of land from its present uses before the prospect of zero population growth can slow increasing demands on U.S. land and water resources.

According to Thomas C. Marcin, an economist with the USDA's Forest Service, U.S. housing requirements to the year 2020 are projected to range between 2.3 and 2.5 million brand new additional dwelling units per year in the 1980s and 2.1 to 2.3 million units per year in the 1990s.[1] Between the years 2000 and 2020, average annual demand is expected to range between 2 and 2.5 million dwelling units. At least 70 percent and as much as 75 percent of the housing demand of the 1980s and

1990s is projected to be for land-devouring single-family houses. Marcin believes that single-family housing could average 1.5 million houses per year, with new apartments ranging between 600,000 units per year in the early 1980s and 400,000 later as the number of young households declines. In summary he projects that the majority of new houses will be built in the West and the South. The Northeast is expected to continue to lose its share of housing production. By 1990 its share may fall to 10 percent. By the year 2000 the South's share of housing production is projected to be 45 percent of the total, the West's 25 percent, and the North Central region about 20 percent. These figures are broadly indicative of where future land consumption pressures are expected to prevail.

At a conservative average cost of $50,000 per dwelling unit, the new housing projected to the year 2000 alone represents an economic potential in excess of $2 trillion. It is my thesis that the protection of our needed natural resources must be achieved in cooperation with and not in competition against the monumental economic and political forces that this new housing and its related private and public support facilities will exert.

If the past is any indication of the future, much of the resulting land use change will take place on prime farm, forest, and water-related land located in existing metropolitan areas.

Some changes will alter places of great scenic beauty while others will simply fill in undeveloped lots in existing subdivisions. In the process, diminished resource availability and productivity will not be the only loss. As land is carved into small parcels there will be a further blocking of our opportunities to walk the land that sustains us, to draw strength and be refreshed by communion with its many natural faces. In our daily routines we will continue to be increasingly confined to the parcels of land we individually own or rent, to public ways, and to the places where we work or go to school. There will also be added pressure on our wetlands and groundwater aquifers, resulting in still further demand on water supply and wastewater management facilities. More roads and schools will be needed.

In short, depending on where they are built, the more than 50 million new dwellings needed to accommodate what may well turn out to be our last wave of population growth will require a significant increase in public and private support facilities.

To get a sense of the land changes that could take place in the next twenty to fifty years, consider the changes worked on the land to accommodate the 81 million increase in U.S. population that took place between 1940 and 1975. In Massachusetts, for example, we went from 35,000 farms covering 2 million acres to 4,700 farms covering 700,000 acres. Another such loss would be disastrous. Over this period our cities swelled over the rings of farms that grew our vegetables, rural areas became suburbs, and once-remote vacation areas such as Cape Cod were developed in ways that defy orderly public and private use.

Clearly the way future growth and change are negotiated onto the land will have enormous social, economic and ecological impact on the affected areas. For some places growth will be a life-enhancing force improving general social and economic well-being while stimulating the positive care of existing natural resources. These areas will take on the appearance of a well-exercised body, with each acre dedicated to appropriate needed functions. My home town of Lincoln, Massachusetts, is undergoing this kind of experience. As each remaining large parcel of unrestricted privately owned land is scheduled for development, great care is given to its possible uses. Creative plans that meet recognized human needs while protecting valued resources are encouraged. As a result, development is taking place while neglected farmland and woodland are given active care and management. A carefully designed system of trails for walking, riding, and cross-country skiing is being established with bicycle paths that meander along tree-lined roads. Care is taken to foster housing that will be suitable for a community of diverse ages, incomes, and social backgrounds. All this is being done with broad public awareness and participation to minimize flaws and omissions. More about Lincoln in the next chapter.

For many other areas, however, growth will continue to be a debilitating force overwhelming natural systems, pitting social group against social group, and requiring municipal services that many towns cannot afford. Much of this flawed development will result from antiquated and abusive zoning practices that give zoning a bad reputation. More will result from sheer ignorance and apathy which, along with greed and stubbornness, account for most U.S. development problems. Fortunately, in a way, we are fast reaching the point where our society can no longer tolerate destructive development. We cannot afford to accommodate the coming 80 millions of Americans at a cost in lost resources comparable to that of the post-1940 wave of growth. It is my hope, as expressed in this book, that such losses can be avoided within the context of our free society.

Although many are now aware that America's growth and technological advance had their price, it wasn't until we were well into the "soaring sixties" that we as a nation began to see the need for corrective and preventative measures to alter the process that was gobbling up our natural resources, impoverishing many of our people, and leaving us with settlement patterns unsuited to our long-run future. By the time we awoke to the fact that all was not well in man-made America in the early 1970s, our air was polluted, our lakes and rivers were fouled, our food production resources were widely separated from our people, and the cost of running the country was beyond our means to pay for it.

Development in the United States has not been evenly distributed and future growth is expected to occur in new patterns of concentration. To understand the ruinous effect of these changes on our resource base and the further threats to natural resources, it is necessary to look beyond gross national and even broad regional figures to see what has been happening in our metropolitan growth nodes and in the development of remote areas. To provide a sense of what is happening in different parts of the country, I have chosen nine areas as examples of the clash of human and natural forces. These include Greater Boston, Massachusetts, where I served as a citizen adviser to the recent wastewater management planning effort. Also included as a tour of the country are Greater Portland, Maine; Cape Cod; the Delaware Valley region, including Philadelphia; the Southwest Florida regional planning area; Greater Denver, Colorado; the San Francisco Bay area; Greater Portland, Oregon; and Greater Des Moines, Iowa. In most of these areas personal experiences have given me a first-hand sense of their growth problems. The following cameos are not intended to present a detailed picture of present and future land use. They are intended to provide a sense of area land resources, growth prospects, potential resource losses, and the overall context in which growth will take place. This view of what is happening in specific areas should provide the background necessary to judge the broad relevance of what has been done in Lincoln, Massachusetts, and other communities we have served. It should also serve to evaluate the merits of the creative process offered in the last chapter.

Greater Boston, Massachusetts

The Greater Boston wastewater management study (under the EPA's planning process) included ninety-two of metropolitan Boston's 101 cities and towns and covers almost 525,000 acres, or 820 square miles. Draining into nine rivers, many of the towns in these basins are suburban or semirural in character. Between 1950 and 1970 areawide population grew 17 percent, from 2.5 million to 2.9 million people. Population growth from 1970 to 1995 is projected to be 320,000, for an increase of 11 percent.

Development within the planning area is most heavily concentrated within an arc bounded by Route 128, a circumferential highway roughly twenty-five miles distant from Boston, which was built after World War II. Having exposed Boston's peripheral towns to development, this highway is largely responsible for the changed patterns of land use on the fringe of Boston between 1950 and 1970. Over that period forested acreage dropped by 11 percent, from 374,000 acres to 331,000 acres, and agricultural land decreased by 56 percent, from 140,000 acres to 62,000 acres. Much of the farmland that was lost to development had been used to produce vegetables for local consumption. In short, the area's Boston-oriented highway network and its Route 128 circumferential highway network facilitated the movement of residential, industrial, and commercial activities away from its core communities. Route 495, an outer circumferential highway completed in the 1970s, is extending the process of fringe development and exposing much of the remainder of the area's forest and farmland to low-density development. As of 1971 this included 62,000 acres of remaining farmland, much of which has since been lost.

Fortunately, although still subject to local control, land in Massachusetts is increasingly subject to conversion under a new statewide growth policy that calls for the revitalization of urban centers and acknowledges the need to protect farmland, wetlands, and other water resources. In most communities there is strict enforcement of the state's environmental code as it relates to the construction of on-site sewage disposal systems and the alteration of inland and coastal wetlands.

The state's new farmland protection program could go a long way toward minimizing future resource losses. In particular, much of Greater Boston's remaining farmland can be protected through participation in the state's preferential farmland assessment program, which keeps property taxes low on qualifying farmland, and our new agricultural development-rights purchase program. Under the latter, farmers may sell the right to develop their land to the state for the difference between what it is worth in the market for development and its value as farmland. Unfortunately this new program is still in a pilot stage, with only $5 million available at this time, and ready accessibility to Greater Boston's remaining farmland will make the purchase of these rights very costly. Nevertheless, the protection of farmland is becoming a recognized priority in this area, and many communities are taking imaginative steps to protect this resource. Moreover, by emphasizing farms that would otherwise be lost to development, even this modest amount of money may help to stabilize Massachusetts agriculture. One of my goals, as a member of the Massachusetts Agricultural Lands Preservation Committee, will be to help our Greater Boston communities use every means possible to save their few remaining acres of farmland. Readers in the nation's vast farmland areas may wonder why there is all the fuss to save these pitifully few acres of farmland. I hope they will learn from our experience and protect theirs while it is still plentiful.

Population growth and changing patterns of land use in the Greater Boston area have also created a serious water shortage. One cause was the Metropolitan District Commission's decision to require that communities tying into the MDC system abandon their local supplies. Initiated as a move to insure the financial success of this system, which brought water from western Massachusetts, this requirement had the effect of encouraging the building of houses on proved aquifers and potential impoundment sites. Now, with the MDC system delivering water beyond its safe yield of 300 million gallons per day, there is pressure to divert water from the Connecticut River to augment the MDC system in order to satisfy the needs of system communities and enable Greater Boston communities not now in the system to join. Again, efforts to ease tensions are being marshaled after much of the needless damage has been done. In this case legislative initiatives are being prepared to enable MDC-served communities to reactivate abandoned resources, to provide technical assistance to communities for the development of water conservation programs, to detect and repair leaks in the MDC system, and to help communities develop new supplies. Whether these initiatives become law or whether they will be adequate to eliminate the need for a major river diversion is not known. What is known is that failure to take into account the long-range water needs of the Greater Boston area has created a major problem for all the communities involved.

So too has the failure of state and local governments to deal with water supply and wastewater management as integral parts of the area's overall hydrology. A particular case in point is Route 128, which runs right along the full length of the Cambridge reservoir system. This important regional resource is exposed to serious contamination from road runoff, including winter road salts and other pollutants, nearby septic systems, and a nearby oil storage tank facility.

My attention was drawn to this situation by Art Barnes, a fellow director of Norumbega, an informal association concerned with regional issues. What we learned about the management of this resource was alarming. First we learned that the state's Department of Public Works felt no responsibility to control runoff of salt (or worse) from Route 128, their main concern being traffic safety. Then we learned that the Metropolitan District Commission, which would be called on to replace the water flows from this resource, did not consider themselves responsible for its protection. Likewise, the four communities of the watershed took no responsibility for protecting the large watershed that feeds the reservoirs. Representatives of major companies with large parking lots near the reservoirs also did not consider the possible impact of their salting practices. Although these meetings did evoke some responses from Cambridge in the form of a crude testing program, I know of no serious efforts to assure the protection of the water quality in these reservoirs. Since Norumbega's efforts have withered, owing to a lack of financial support, I suspect that all interest has lapsed.

As a citizen adviser to the Greater Boston area's wastewater management planning program, I struggled for two years to have water supply added as a consideration, pointing to situations such as the plight of the Cambridge reservoirs, with little result. I fear that collapse of this system will add a needless impetus to diversion of the Connecticut River so that the MDC will be able to make up for its possible loss.

The Cambridge reservoirs are but one example of the way we fail to recognize, let alone protect, important water resources. There have been many cases in the Greater Boston area of groundwater wells lost because of careless storage of road salt and unplanned housing development. We must become aware of our vital resources and learn to protect them.

Portland, Maine

Greater Portland is the fastest-growing regional area in Maine. Comprised of twenty-two cities and towns covering over 500,-000 acres, this region has a population that is expected to rise by 32 percent, from 189,000 to 250,000, by the year 2000. Although this growth may translate into only 60,000 to 80,000 more houses, there is great concern that it could trigger a significant rise in property taxes and adversely affect local farming. Much of the concern stems from Maine's severe limitations for on-site sewage disposal and the high cost of sewerage to the existing population.

Maine suffers from shallow depth to bedrock and poorly draining soils, particularly on the coast and in the Greater Portland area, where rapid growth prevails. The severity of Maine's soil limitations for on-site sewage disposal is evident in the estimate that the conventional plumbing code based on federal recommendations in effect from 1967 to 1974 technically blocked development in over 85 percent of the state.

Recognizing that new technologies such as mounding, the separation of systems for different quality wastewaters, and nondischarging systems such as composting toilets can, if properly engineered, safely provide suitable on-site sewage disposal on shallow soils, Maine adopted a new plumbing code in 1974 that required only 15 inches of on-site permeable soils for a septic system instead of the 48 inches previously required. This has had the effect of opening 85 percent of the state to low-density development. As a result the Greater Portland area is exposed to scattered growth with pockets of density that may require later sewerage if the plumbing code is not properly enforced at the local level.

The Greater Portland area's growth problems are compounded by failing septic systems from past development and the conversion of summer homes to year-round homes, leading to still further septic system failures. As a result several communities are planning sewer lines that will expose farmland and salt water marshes to unwanted development. In Cape Elizabeth, which is just south of Portland, these issues are now being confronted in an imaginative way. There consideration is being given to the possibility of applying the concept of transferable development rights to concentrate new development along the proposed sewer line extension. Since sewerage will enable higher densities on the land served by the sewers, the principle is to permit such increases only with the purchase of development rights from resource land the town wants to protect. In this way the town would recapture any increased density windfall that would otherwise accrue to landowners along the proposed sewer line and harness it to the protection of farmland and other land desired to be kept in its present use. This is the first time that I have come across this approach and will be anxious to see if it can control the location of the 1,500 new houses expected to be built by the year 2000. As to the protection of marshes from development threatened by abutting sewer lines, it has been suggested to the Cape Elizabeth planners that they consider advance prohibition of sewer connections from these areas. Precedent for such limitations already exists in places like Block Island, Rhode Island.

Several communities in the Greater Portland area share Maine's growing concern over the loss of its farmland to development. A case in point is the inland town of Gorham. With most of the town's farmland zoned for 60,000-square-foot house lots in 1976, and with neighboring towns changing to two-acre or greater residential lot zoning, Gorham farmers organized to prevent scattered development that could lead to the collapse of their local agriculture. When I was there in 1977, a blue-ribbon committee of farmers had just recommended to the Gorham Town Council that local farmland be rezoned to five-acre house lots and that all possible methods, including the purchase of agricultural rights and agricultural zoning, be considered for the protection of the town's farmland.

Although it's too early to tell whether these measures will work, it is clear that at least some Maine farmers are going to resist the loss of their farmland to development. But unless there are strong clustering provisions, I fear that five-acre farmland zoning will only hasten the collapse of local commercial agriculture. Moreover, it will not be easy to convince Maine's population of close to one million that it should commit itself to purchase development rights on the state's one million acres of prime farmland, including over 300,000 acres of cropland. Nevertheless, the farmland problem has been perceived in the Greater Portland area and there is good reason to believe that losses will be reduced.

Two former serious conflicts between growth and natural resources in the Greater Portland area have been resolved through extensive application of Maine's shore-line and resource-protection zoning designed to prohibit encroachment on the state's fragile and sensitive areas. By declaring these areas out of bounds to development, they should prevent future estuarine, dune, and wetlands destruction of the sort that has characterized so much of coastal Maine's early development.

The state of Maine and its Greater Portland communities are very much aware of the conflicts that growth poses to their natural resources. Much of the planning to guide Greater Portland's expected growth away from valued natural resources has been started. Staff planners for the area's Council of Governments are fully up to date in the skills required to help communities plan for their future. Local planning boards and conservation commission members take their work seriously. Active as an adviser to owners of several large parcels in Cape Elizabeth, I am particularly impressed with their dedication and planning skills. There it is recognized that the future will depend on the cooperative efforts of large landowners and representatives of their town as they work to implement plans in ways that are fair to all concerned.

Cape Cod, Massachusetts

Cape Cod is a peninsula extending 90 miles seaward along the Massachusetts coast. The total area of the region is only 253,-000 acres, of which 64,000 were already developed for residential and commercial use by 1975. Of the balance 61,000 acres were reserved open space, for example, the National Seashore, Otis Air Force Base, and town conservation land; 93,000 acres were considered vacant; and 35,000 acres were protected as wetlands and sand areas.

Politically the Cape is comprised of fifteen towns with a year-round population of 128,000. Population has surged to this level from 45,000 in 1950 and is projected to reach 190,000 by 1995. Summer population, including year-round residents, has exploded from 155,000 in 1950 to 380,000 in 1975 and is projected to reach 570,000 by 1995. With many of the present summer cottages being converted into year-round dwellings, the Cape is essentially under development siege.

The major land use change projected for 1995 is the conversion of 52,000 acres of presently "vacant" land into houses. This means that an amount of land comparable to that developed in the last 350 years will be developed over the next twenty years, leaving few options for the twenty-first century. Clearly, any of the 22,754 acres that the Cape had in farmland in 1971 that are still not developed in 1979 will be under severe development pressure. Even the area's famous cranberry bogs are subject to drainage and development.

Perhaps the most serious growth problem confronting the Cape will be the protection of groundwater and the avoidance of salt water intrusion and pond eutrophication. Essentially a homogenous band of sandy gravel, the Cape's subsurface soils function as a continuous aquifer holding fresh water that floats as a lens on heavier salt water. This essential resource is subject to gradual contamination from sources such as failing septic systems and leaching from "sanitary" landfills. It is also vulnerable to salt water intrusion as groundwater is removed from its normal hydrological cycle and flushed as sewerage into ocean outfalls required to accommodate dense development. Indeed, protection of the Cape's groundwater for drinking is a primary concern of the Cape's fifteen communities. I wouldn't be surprised to see the need for imported water bringing still further pressure for diverting the Connecticut River.

Fortunately the Cape is a much-loved piece of land with many caring people who are able and willing to participate in its growth-guiding process. The economic pressures on the area's undeveloped land, however, are enormous. Clearly this is one place where careful planning will be required in order to accommodate demand in the area's limited land mass without destroying the fragile environmental systems that support the enormous investments that have already been made.

Delaware Valley Region, Including Philadelphia

The Delaware Valley region encompasses Berks, Bucks, Chester, Delaware, Montgomery, and Philadelphia counties, approximately half of Schuylkill County, and a small portion of Lebanon County. This area covers 2.2 million acres, roughly one one-thousandth of the land mass of the United States, and supports 4.3 million people, or close to 2 percent of our population. By the year 2000 the area's population is expected to swell by 16 percent to 5 million. This translates into 200,000 to 300,000 new homes.

The Delaware Valley region's wastewater management plan describes the area as one of great variety spanning "four physiographic provinces, from the level Coastal Plain to the intensely folded valley and ridge province. Geologically complex, it includes extensive coal and limestone formations, valuable resources with unique water quality and land use planning implications. Soils are correspondingly varied; there are some with severe limitations for on-lot disposal systems, others with high erosion potential, and large amounts which rank among the world's finest agricultural soils."

Of the area's 2.2 million acres, major uses in 1970 included 956,000 acres in agriculture, 780,000 acres in forest and recreation or undeveloped use, and 269,000 acres in residential use. Manufacturing, transportation, utilities, and mining accounted for 145,000 acres.

As to land use patterns, the area's wastewater management report states: "Before 1950, most urban and industrial development in the Study Area had occurred along the Delaware River. During the 1950's, however, urbanized, industrial areas began to spring up along the rail and highway corridors leading westward, in many cases attracting industry from older urban centers. Suburban residential development accelerated as well, and the 1960's were marked by 'urban sprawl.' More recently, the shopping mall and the industrial park have become popular development concepts, taking advantage of readily available, less expensive land, an extensive highway network, and ample markets and labor force. These regional growth centers have, in turn, encouraged further growth in service industries and suburban residential land use." This well describes what's happening in many places besides the Delaware Valley region. In any case, it is projected that the area's expected growth of 750,000 people by the year 2000 will require the conversion of 100,000 acres, of which some 50 to 75 percent is now in agricultural production.

My only direct contact with this region was through the Schuylkill Valley Nature Center. Invited in later 1978 to advise them regarding the protection of an 85-acre piece of farmland abutting their facility, I took the opportunity to urge their participation in the protection of farmland on the urban fringe of Philadelphia. Considering the area's projections, I think that the prospective loss of an additional 50,000 to 75,000 acres of productive farmland is more than our nation (let alone the region) can afford. As a member of the Northeast Association of State Departments of Agriculture, I know that Pennsylvania is actively interested in saving its remaining farmland. The question is how many more acres will be lost before effective state and local programs stem the loss. Unlike Cape Cod the area seems to have ample nonfarm land to accommodate its future growth.

Southwest Florida

The Southwest Florida Regional Planning Area, comprised of six counties covering 4.3 million acres, is one of the nation's fastest growing areas. Between 1950 and 1976 the region's population jumped from 71,255 people to 458,053, for an increase of 525 percent. This population is expected to more than double by the year 2000. In 1975, 2.1 million acres, or 54.5 percent of the total, were in agriculture, with over 1.5 million acres used for livestock, close to 300,000 acres for crops, and the balance as woodland. The remaining land uses were urban, 10.6 percent; open space, 20.7 percent; and vacant, 14.2 percent.

As described in the area's 1978 Land Use Policy Plan: "Southwest Florida is characterized by a flat topography, poorly-drained soils, and a subtropical climate, with an average annual rainfall of 53 inches. The environment of the area is highly dependent upon an extensive and intricate web of estuarine, freshwater wetland and groundwater systems. The region's coastal zone and inland areas have some of the most desirable water-related natural resources remaining in the United States. Broad expanses of water, rich estuarines, accessible islands, and warm climate have combined as a major force stimulating this region's fast growth over the past 25 years. This rapid growth has established the character of the region's land use, its population, and its planning for future needs."

Unlike in the northeast states, public planning and administration in Florida is highly concentrated, with the Southwest Florida region managed by six county and thirteen municipal governments. Growth is such an important part of area activities that its management appears to be the dominant government activity.

Since most of Southwest Florida's growth is oriented toward the area's coastal regions, major conflicts revolve around the protection of fragile ecosystems. The stakes are high, with over 160 subdivisions covering 525,000 acres already platted for over one million lots, enough to accommodate an increase in population of over 3.2 million people. This premature land preparation confronts the area with a future of unserviceable and environmentally unsuitable residential locations. Water supply is a major problem; the limited surface and groundwater sources are recognized as inadequate to meet the needs of the additional dwelling unit potential even if all the fresh water sources in the region are utilized.

In addition to the area's major water supply and fragile ecosystem growth conflicts, potential conflict is seen to exist between agricultural lands and population expansion, particularly on the urban fringes. There is a need to modify platted lots to better suit population needs and protect natural systems. Historical and archeological sites are also threatened. Expansion of transportation systems threatens established neighborhoods and fragile areas. Competition between municipalities leads to planning based on duplicate expectations of attracting available growth. In addition unusual conflicts result from the need to limit growth to possible storm evacuation capabilities.

Based on my participation in the Conservation Foundation's efforts in the area's Rookery Bay protection planning program in the early 1970s, my principal observation relates to the relatively large scale of the area's development problems. Large ecosystems are threatened by large-scale developers working within a large governmental framework. Nothing seems small scale in Florida. Protected areas such as Big Cyprus, Corkscrew Swamp, and the Everglades Park are enormous in comparison to most comparable areas in the Northeast. With most land use battles fought in the county and municipal planning offices there seems little place to work out the smaller issues that soften the impact of a development and ease it onto the land. I wasn't surprised in 1976 to find that Sanibel's new municipal ordinance, for example, left that beautiful island with no real provision for needed low- and moderate-income housing and no process to deal with the owners of small lots converted to low-density development to protect low-lying wetlands. Nevertheless, I am much impressed with the attention given growth issues, the sharpness of the concepts and programs designed to control growth, and the innovative use of such management tools as capital improvement programming, impact fees, special taxing mechanisms, and formal impact assessments on developments exceeding established size thresholds.

As I observe Southwest Florida cope with its growth problems, I believe it may be able to protect its fragile resources and provide needed services and protection for its citizens better than continue its role as a national food supplier. Also of concern are such small-scale needs as special housing and the interests of owners of small lots preempted from development. Unlike the preceding East Coast area examples, there is no long tradition of land ownership and stewardship with which to work. Broadly seen as a commodity to be exploited, valuable resource land in Southwest Florida will be difficult to protect without full recognition of its highest potential development value.

Denver, Colorado

The Greater Denver planning area covers 3.1 million acres. In 1977 this five-county region had a population of 1.5 million people, which was projected to grow by 56 percent to 2.35 million by the year 2000. In the area's planning literature, this is seen as dumping a city the size of Washington, D.C., on the Denver metropolitan area over the next twenty years. This is about the same amount of growth experienced by the area between 1950 and 1970, when it grew at 2.5 times the national average.

Important farmland has already been lost to development. A good description of Colorado's overall growth conflicts is contained in Congressman Frank E. Evans's testimony given in 1977 during hearings on the proposed National Agricultural Land Policy Act. In this testimony he described Colorado as having 3 million acres of irrigated cropland lying along the valleys of the Arkansas, Colorado, Rio Grande, and Platte rivers. This land is serviced by 3,000 individual irrigation companies. Competition for water and development land in Boulder, Weld, Lamar, Adams, Mesa, and Pueblo is seen as intense. From 1960 to 1970 Colorado lost 189,000 acres of irrigated cropland and gained 60,000 acres of urban development. In his testimony Congressman Evans suggests "that competition to date has been small scale compared to the future land and water demands of energy development in the Rocky Mountain West. As 62 billion tons of recoverable coal reserves plus 1,800 billion barrels of shale oil begin to be developed, thousands upon thousands of new residents will be attracted to the region and, as a consequence, an estimated 70,000 to 100,000 acre feet of water will have to be diverted from agriculture."

Another major growth problem in areas surrounding Denver is the speculative development of fragile mountain areas into ski resorts. I recall being invited in 1974 to Summit County, Colorado, to keynote a conference of developers and environmentalists on the future of that 10,000-foot-high area. The Eisenhower Tunnel had recently been opened, exposing the area to easy access from places like Boulder and Denver. What I remember most about that trip is the great length of time it takes to grow vegetation at those high elevations. Areas scorched by fire over fifty years earlier were still barren. I also remember the steep cuts in the mountains for road access to perched house sites, the danger of mud slides, and the sense that it all didn't matter because the lots were being bought by speculators and would never be developed. John Denver's song,

"Rocky Mountain High," was popular that summer and there was a feeling that the environmental war was being fought in Summit County, an area that had waited a long time since the exhaustion of the gold mines for economic attention and wasn't about to miss out on the winter recreation boom knocking at its door. And yet, even in 1974, people were wondering about the effects of introducing so much auto and fireplace exhaust at high altitudes on the downwind climate of places like Denver. At that time the concern was one of altering rain patterns by warming the atmosphere. By now I would assume the concern is acid rain and smog.

San Francisco, California

The San Francisco Bay area, along with much of the rest of California, is a prime example of a place where virulent population growth poses a serious threat to vital land and water resources. It is also a place that has set forth a bold program to accommodate expected growth without furthering the attrition of farmland and aquifers that characterized its dramatic post–World War II sprawl. With so much of our country's food coming from California, it is with keen interest that we will be monitoring the success of California's urban development strategy to keep the 4 to 8 million population growth expected by the year 2000 from sprawling across the farms that feed us. It will be more than interesting to see if California, as the most urban state in the nation, can retain agriculture as its number one business and continue its role as a major food exporting state. Success will depend on the creation of incentives that succeed in fostering growth in accord with the state's three priorities of reviving and maintaining existing urban areas—both cities and suburbs; developing vacant land that is within existing urban areas and presently served by streets, water, sewer, and other public services; and, where land outside existing urban areas must be utilized, developing only land that is immediately adjacent to these areas.

Success should mean putting an end to the daily destruction of an estimated 475 acres of prime California agricultural land.

Frankly, I suspect that it will not be an easy matter to reverse California's growth dynamics without compensating farmland owners and those of other lands of public conservation interest for their lost financial gains from development. I fear that California's urban development strategy will turn out to be a Maginot Line that will be circumvented by farmland owners and others who have a chance to profit through development and that California will succumb to these losses as competing economic activities overcome the legal and political barriers protecting threatened farm and other resource land. California's expected growth between now and the year 2000 represents 10 to 20 percent of America's overall projected growth over this same period. In my opinion this will not be an easy force to contain within, or even close to, California's present urban areas.

With these doubts in mind, let's take a quick look at California's San Francisco Bay area.

This area is comprised of nine counties covering 4.5 million acres. In 1975 the Bay area's population totaled close to 4.7 million people occupying 1.8 million dwelling units. By the year 2000 this population is projected to grow by 27 percent to 6 million residents living in 2.6 million units. According to the Association of Bay Area Governments (ABAG), the projected growth will occur on 312,440 acres of land designated as being "policy developable" and will not adversely affect 3.7 million acres designated as unusable for development. These latter acres consist of "open public lands and other areas where cities and counties have taken action either to exclude them from development or to defer development beyond the time period of the projection."

The 312,000 acres of "policy developable" land in the projection system are divided into prime and secondary: "land zoned for development where sewer and water services exist or are committed to a level sufficient to accommodate new development" and "land where zoning allows development but with recognized constraints due to lack of sewer or water service or physical constraints such as flooding and steep slopes."

The Bay area's wastewater management strategy, in short, is linked to California's urban development strategy, which calls for urban infilling and rebuilding before urban areas are allowed to spread. I agree that development of an urban density can be effectively channeled through careful public investment in roads, sewers, schools, and other public facilities. I believe, however, that it is quite another matter to guide low-density growth away from important resource land. It's hard for me to see, for example, how California's broad brush urban strategy will prevent the conversion of small farms into low-density development relying on on-site sewage disposal and local water supply.

In February 1978 I had the pleasure of experiencing the San Francisco area's growth conflicts as a guest of the Trust for Public Land. As principal contributor to a two-day conference attended by members of land trusts from all over the state as well as other western states and Florida, I was struck by the reception given to Lincoln's approach to dealing with growth. After the conference I was taken to Napa and other areas where important resource parcels are being lost to development. Since that trip a representative of TPL has come to tour Lincoln as part of his research for a training manual. In addition representatives of several California communities have contacted me for greater detail on our approach. The relevance of the Lincoln experience to the California situation was recently acknowledged by Joseph Petrillo, head of California's Coastal Conservancy at a national conference on federal land acquisition sponsored jointly by the Lincoln Institute of Land Policy and the Conservation Foundation.

Portland, Oregon

In selecting areas to spotlight, I had to include Oregon for its pioneering land management program which promises to contain most of the state's future growth within well-defined urban bounds. According to William K. Reilly, president of the Conservation Foundation, "the strength of Oregon's program is in the combination of its Agricultural Lands and Urbanization goals." Each of Oregon's 544 cities is required, in cooperation with county government, to draw an "urban growth boundary" around its "urban" and "urbanizable" lands. The area encompassed by this boundary is to be sufficient to accommodate growth needs, identified according to the state's criteria, for fifteen to twenty years. Lands outside the urban growth boundary are "rural lands." The state's policy is that on rural lands, all Class I–IV soils (as classified by the U.S. Soil Conservation Service) are to be zoned for "exclusive farm use" and may not be converted to urban uses. The state's standards for farm use zoning are designed to keep large blocks of farmland in production, rather than merely checkerboarded parcels.

I first learned of the Oregon plan in 1974 when members of the Conservation Foundation came to Boston with area representatives as part of its introduction of its milestone book, *The Use of Land.* I caught up with its progress in late 1977 when I had the good fortune of being introduced to Henry R. Richmond, director of 1000 Friends of Oregon. Henry was in Boston visiting a mutual friend when I arrived from witnessing our governor's signing of a $5 million development rights acquisition bill to save Massachusetts farmland. I'll never forget Henry's frank response when I related this to him; he believed that our approach would bankrupt Massachusetts. He then gave me a copy of his two-year progress report that recorded the major legal decisions supporting Oregon's approach to orderly growth. It revealed why Henry thinks we're a bit mad in Massachusetts to spend money to save farmland. His report states, for example, that "because nearly all of the two million acre floor of the Willamette Valley is Class I–IV soils, the state's new policy means that counties will rezone nearly all of the valley floor from no zoning or zoning for 3–5 acre ranchette subdivisions to EFU (Exclusive Farm Use)."

Although it's easy for me to argue that what works in Oregon need not work in Massachusetts, I must confess that I would like to see us determine which approach might be the best to follow. Oregon seems to have accomplished through noncompensatory zoning what would otherwise have cost the public an estimated $5 billion. Tom McCall relates how he was informed in a Senate Interior Committee hearing that it would cost an estimated trillion dollars to save U.S. farmland alone on a compensatory basis.[2] Clifford Hansen, who made this estimate, went on to argue that once the door to compensatory zoning was opened to save farmland, the precedent would be used by owners of land of every description to be compensated for being denied the right to achieve higher development value. In short, there is a school of thought that fears that compensating landowners who for the public good are denied the right to convert their land from one use to another will lead to national bankruptcy. If so, the time to have this out is now as development-rights acquisition programs are emerging all around the country.

The same holds true for the viability of noncompensatory zoning. After all, twenty Oregon localities have filed suit to have the basic land use law of the state of Oregon declared unconstitutional. If Oregon's law is struck down, can it be long before California's similar approach is also declared unconstitutional? Frankly I am leery of both approaches. Their principal appeal is their simplicity and the ability to impose them from on high. In one case the government essentially pays protection money to prevent unwanted land conversion; in the other it simply prohibits unwanted change. If events prove that we can't afford the former and the second is unconstitutional, what will we do? Clearly we must develop a more creative and more reliable set of options to deal effectively with change as it takes place.

The Columbia Region Association of Governments, in their wastewater management plans for the Greater Portland area, give us a quick overview of impending growth conflicts. Their principal planning area includes three counties covering close to 2 million acres, of which 1.1 million are publicly owned. The population of this area in 1975 totaled 940,800, or close to 42 percent of Oregon's entire population. The area's population is projected to grow by 42 percent to 1.35 million by the year 2000, with 1.2 million projected population expected to live in areas confined within urban growth boundaries.

Originally the urban area was scheduled to expand by 157 square miles to accommodate projected population growth. I was impressed to learn from Henry Richmond's report that 1000 Friends of Oregon had successfully challenged this proposed expansion as excessive. Through an appeal to the Oregon Land Conservation and Development Commission (LCDC), 1000 Friends of Oregon were successful in reducing the planned urban expansion to 39 square miles. The appeal was won with the argument "that the sprawling CRAG plan would have cost taxpayers $100 million more to build and maintain sewer lines, streets and water mains than if the plan complied with LCDC's Urbanization Goal."[3]

As long as the courts support this kind of planning, the Greater Portland area should readily be able to shield its productive land and water resources from population growth. In addition to suggesting possible fall-back approaches, nevertheless, it is hoped that creative development of the sort described in later chapters can be helpful in negotiating onto the land the 400,000 additional people expected in the Greater Portland area by the year 2000.

Des Moines, Iowa

The Greater Des Moines area is another where my principal data source is the regional planning agency conducting area-wide wastewater management planning. The Des Moines region is comprised of twenty-three municipalities within most of Polk County and portions of Dallas and Warren counties. The area covers 513,000 acres, of which 428,000 are in agriculture, including 350,000 acres of the most productive soils in the world. The population of the area was 315,000 in 1970 and is projected to grow to 400,000 by the year 2000.

Twenty of twenty-six local jurisdictions have comprehensive plans and zoning ordinances. Based on these plans the Des Moines regional agency expects projected growth to settle largely in the urban core of Des Moines with outlying communities anticipating 40 percent of the total growth. All in all it is expected that 32,873 acres will be shifted from pasture, forest, vacant, and cropland uses to residential and urban uses.

To the extent that good cropland lies along existing roads and that sewer lines are run along these roads to service failing septic systems, pressure can be expected to convert frontage acres into house lots, particularly where sewer assessments are made on an availability basis. This is the same conversion pressure that poses a threat to marshes in Maine and other coastal areas. Here, too, it is a pressure that needs to be relieved in a fair and equitable manner through appropriate planning and implementation.

The growth problems confronting Des Moines go way beyond the possible loss of a few thousand acres of choice cropland and the correction of existing wastewater problems. As the area's economic base broadens beyond agriculture, new needs and conflicts are bound to arise. One planning report expresses the thought that "with the implementation of the plan the Des Moines area can market itself as a metropolitan area which has come to grips with the problems of wastewater management." Looking ahead one can't help but wonder if places like Des Moines aren't setting themselves up for accelerated growth as more people include assured food supply in their settlement considerations. As Des Moines grows as a metropolitan center, isn't it possible that much of the area's growth will want to live on individual ranchettes? If so, isn't there a danger that greater losses of our best farmland from intensive cultivation will result? In the absence of either a noncompensatory zoning program like Oregon's or compensatory programs like those in effect in New York, New Jersey, Connecticut, Massachusetts, and Washington—or some other creative approach to guiding growth—it's really impossible to predict the long-range availability of Greater Des Moines's 428,000 acres of farmland to agriculture. After all, only 95,000 acres, or 16.5 percent of the area, are not now dedicated to agriculture. Any significant population growth is bound to eat into the area's agricultural base.

In any case, as metropolitan growth sets in around Des Moines, development problems comparable to those of the East are likely to occur. The following chapters may provide examples and suggestions that will be helpful in dealing with growth in Des Moines and the other eight areas sketched in this quick sampling of America's prospective growth conflicts.

Assuming that these nine regional sketches are representative of the resource pressures confronting America, it should be apparent that we have just begun to see the planning and management effort that will be needed to establish a working equilibrium between ourselves and our country's natural systems. It should also be apparent that there is no assurance that our diverse ways of dealing with our nation's land use conflicts will produce the needed balance. To the contrary, there is every indication that the failure to plan and to balance land conversion in America will lead to cumulative losses; these in turn will result in dreadful shortages and regional competition for food, water, and energy. Moreover, there is every reason to believe that our expected growth will make it increasingly difficult for the United States to cope with its own resource requirements let alone play a leadership role in a needed global drive toward population equilibrium.

CHAPTER FOUR

Land Conversion in Lincoln, Massachusetts

LINCOLN IS A rural suburb located thirteen miles from Boston, on its western fringe. Bordered by Lexington, Bedford, Concord, Sudbury, and Weston, Lincoln has a long history that predates the American Revolution. It was in Lincoln that Paul Revere was captured by the British as he rode to Concord to sound the alarm. A community of 5,200 people, Lincoln covers 9,500 acres and governs itself under a town meeting form of government with elected unpaid officials. Under this form of government all zoning and budgeting decisions are made by registered voters at annual and special town meetings.

David Morine, the Nature Conservancy's director of acquisitions and a personal friend, believes that Lincoln is the best example of community land use planning in the United States. To a great extent, David's proddings to document the Lincoln land use story prompted this book.

Lincoln is home to me. It is a growing community of people of different backgrounds, means, and interests struggling together to live in some sort of harmony with the town's natural systems while playing a supportive role in its metropolitan region. The people of Lincoln have a long tradition of giving high priority to land use matters. This chapter is the story of their achievements.

I must emphasize that this is not a chronicle of the countless contributions of all the people who have shaped Lincoln's past and given sure direction to its future. That would require several volumes. Rather this chapter is an effort to present my perceptions of what took place over sixteen years of my involvement in Lincoln's land use affairs. Beyond that it is an effort to distill and present the central issues and events that have moved the town to take an active role in shaping the future of its undeveloped land. The planning steps and implementation techniques applied in several representative cases are described to permit their serious consideration for possible application elsewhere. Individuals are mentioned only when necessary for detail and continuity.

When my wife and I moved to Lincoln in 1961, the town's residential zoning was essentially limited to two-acre house lots. This meant that every new dwelling unit required the conversion of two acres of undeveloped land to residential use. Although there had been considerable development in the late 1940s and 1950s, the town was still largely open although developing at the rate of fifty houses per year.

Ginny and I weren't particularly land or even small-town conscious when we moved to Lincoln from our little apartment in Cambridge. As we drove to Lincoln we were aware of the many woods and open fields but it never occurred to us that they might change or that I would spend much of the next sixteen years trying to save them. Sometimes I wonder if people still choose communities as naively as we did.

Shortly thereafter I became aware that Lincoln's open fields could not be taken for granted. We were at a neighborhood barbecue when it was mentioned that the lovely abutting farm field which backed up to Massachusetts Audubon's Drumlin Farm was on the market. At the time it looked as if the field was to be subdivided into two-acre house lots. As the conversation moved on, I came to wonder how much of Lincoln's undeveloped land was subject to unexpected change. Fortunately, Massachusetts Audubon was able to purchase the neighboring field and it continues in agriculture today. But the plight of that field changed my life, because commuter train conversation about this situation with the town moderator soon led to my unexpected appointment in 1963 to Lincoln's five-year-old Conservation Commission.

I still remember bringing home from my first meeting a handbook for conservation commissioners and a copy of the town's first master plan, known as the Braun-Eliot Report, which had been published in 1958. In essence, the handbook described the role of conservation commissions in Massachusetts; its purpose was to identify and protect the town's natural resources. The Braun-Eliot Report noted that the number of dwelling units had more than doubled between 1946 and 1957, from 425 to 933. It identified 3,728 acres of "vacant land," of which 491 acres were considered as wet, to be protected as a swamp belt. Of the balance 1,441 acres were proposed for diverse public uses, including 215 acres to be purchased by the town to establish a town forest and protect the banks of Sandy Pond, the town's reservoir; 315 acres to be acquired by the state for outdoor recreation; and another 218 acres to be protected for trails, greenways, and other open space. The plan went on to suggest that at the then rate of fifty new houses per year, the remaining 2,287 vacant acres could be expected to be fully developed into 850 house lots by 1978, resulting in a stabilization of the town's population at 6,000. The report did not estimate the value of the land to be protected or the fiscal implications of its purchase. Although the report did not identify specific pieces of undeveloped land by owner and present use or suggest when it might be placed on the market, it represented a charge to the Conservation Commission to work for the protection of 748 of the town's 3,728 acres of so-called vacant land.

Although looking back one can see that not all of the undeveloped land would have come onto the market by 1978, it is quite clear that perhaps as many as 700 houses would have sprawled over the 1,400 acres that have since been saved by the Conservation Commission, Land Trust, and Rural Land Foundation, and that the prophecy of a possible end to open land in Lincoln would have been fulfilled. Instead, more than 400 dwelling units have been built, apartments in existing houses have accommodated an additional seventy-five families, and the Lincoln population is now expected to stabilize at perhaps 7,500 people while Lincoln's open fields, important woods, and connectors will have been protected. But I'm getting ahead of myself. Back in 1963 the sale of private undeveloped land resulted only in houses on two-acre lots.

After reading the Braun-Eliot Report, I was moved to call Town Hall and find out who owned the undeveloped land in Lincoln; this might be a guide to when parcels would be offered for sale. My specific question was: Who owned fifteen or more acres of land and how much did each of these owners hold? I was surprised to find a list of fifteen people who held much of the undeveloped land in town.

I remember going to my second Conservation Commission meeting with this list and the animated discussion that it triggered. It was suddenly clear that important pieces of undeveloped land were owned by elderly people and that much of it could be expected to appear on the market in the near future. The future of Lincoln's undeveloped land was no longer an abstract problem. It was linked to specific pieces owned by specific owners who had specific financial needs. Soon it was clear that Lincoln had a major open space problem that required immediate townwide attention. The cold realities that began to set in included the realization that the town could not count on the state to protect the 315 acres designated for its protection in the Braun-Eliot Report.

As I considered this problem it occurred to me that much of Lincoln's endangered land could be protected through direct purchase if Lincoln were prepared to fund the purchase over time through bond issues, as it did for its school construction —particularly if it could obtain the 75 percent state and federal funding assistance that was then available. I ran some calculations that showed the feasibility of purchasing 1,000 acres for

$2 million with $1.5 million available state and federal funding. These showed that, bonded over twenty years at 4 percent interest, the cost of paying off the $500,000 balance would be $45,000 the first year, scaling down to $25,000 the last year. At the time the town's private property was assessed for $13.6 million. This meant that each dollar on the tax rate raised $13,600 and that the average house was assessed for close to $12,500. As a result it looked as though such an acquisition program would raise the tax levy an average of $35,000, or approximately $2.50 on the tax rate, and would cost the average family around $31 per year. That seemed a reasonable amount to accomplish the job to be done, particularly when the Braun-Eliot Report had revealed that new housing in Lincoln was falling far short of paying its share of municipal services. In fact this report had calculated that an average house with one child in school paid its way but that each additional child in school created a burden of $345. Since the average new home at that time had several students, and school costs were on the rise, it was easy to show that the 500 new houses that might otherwise be built on the 1,000 acres to be saved would raise taxes a great deal more than the cost of saving the land. In short it was now known that Lincoln had an open space problem and that practical solutions to the problem were available.

The suggestion that the town buy a thousand acres was a bit bold in 1963. To be sure, the 1958 Braun-Eliot Report had recommended town purchase of 215 acres, many of them wet. But the land acquisitions now being considered involved a much larger fiscal commitment and required a great deal of citizen support. I well remember trying it out on Warren Flint one Sunday morning. You need to know that Warren was then and still is the touchstone of Lincoln's land use conscience. He and his family go way back in Lincoln history. The land he lives on was granted to his family when Massachusetts was a colony. Like his father, and generations of grandfathers, Warren has farmed the Flint family land in Lincoln. Active in town politics and church matters, the Flints have always had an important

say in what makes sense for Lincoln. I remember Warren reply-
ing something like, "That's quite an idea," or "You've got
something there." Anyhow, the idea caught on and became part
of the thinking that went into a comprehensive planning effort
previously initiated by the selectmen and Planning Board to
deal with the wave of change that they too had seen coming.

The use of land has long been a matter of broad concern to
Lincoln citizens. Although outside planning consultants have
been retained from time to time since the 1950s for their particular expertise, there has always been a great deal of close citizen
participation in the planning process. This was particularly true
in the planning effort completed in 1965 that set detailed goals
to be achieved by 1970, based on a careful Conservation Commission and neighborhood survey of land to be protected. Since
the town's soils had not yet been surveyed for development
limitations and the world food crisis was still a thing of the
future, the criteria for protection were pretty much limited to
the obvious. Aesthetics, such outdoor fun activities as skating,
sledding, riding, and walking, and intuition led to the identification of 800 to 1,400 acres of land to be considered for preservation. By this time the economics of acquiring open space were
pretty well understood and the report called for the purchase
of 800 acres. Included were Lincoln's open fields, the land
around the town's water supply at Sandy Pond, special hills and
ponds, and, to be sure, trail connectors.

By the time the By-70 report was published, changes in the
Conservation Commission's membership resulted in my being
elected chairman. By this time the town had already purchased
four parcels totaling 112 acres at a gross cost of $117,000. Reim-
bursements of $35,750 had reduced the net cost to the town to
$81,250.

The commission's pace picked up in 1966 when four parcels
totaling 70 acres were acquired for a gross sum of $125,850.
Reimbursements of $82,637 reduced the town's cost to the
manageable sum of $43,213. I can recall getting up at Town
Meeting to propose each of the acquisitions and finding little

opposition. To be sure, there was a fair amount of time spent negotiating with owners, walking the land, describing it at public hearings, and filling out grant applications. Yet it looked as if Lincoln had invented the ultimate response to the sprawl that was threatening our lovely undeveloped land. The answer very simply, or so it seemed, was to purchase it before it reached the market.

But Lincoln was still a Yankee town and land was coming on the market at an ever-increasing rate. The question just beneath the surface was, Could we really afford to buy all the undeveloped land that our planning indicated should be protected? Fortunately, and I mean fortunately, it was not long before another way to save land was created.

It was still 1966 when a group of conservation-minded citizens learned that the 109-acre Wheeler Farm with its two colonial farmhouses was going to be sold for $305,000. Rather than involving the Conservation Commission and asking the town to undertake another large expenditure, one that would have exceeded all the prior conservation purchases and would probably not have passed with a necessary two-thirds vote at Town Meeting, they saw that not all the farm needed protection. They set out to find a way of satisfying the financial interests of the owners without overwhelming the land with new development.

Made up of rolling fields and wooded slopes, this farm has an old colonial road running through it. Along this road five British soldiers killed along the Battle Road between Lexington and Concord at the beginning of the Revolution were taken to the Lincoln burial ground, now the Lincoln Cemetery. It was important that this old stone-wall-bordered road, abandoned but intact in our woods, and the land around the cemetery be protected. Development proposed to the Wheelers would have resulted in as many as forty new houses with paved roads covering the entire site. The Wheelers loved their land and were eager to cooperate with the Lincoln conservationists who proposed that the land not be developed in the ordinary way.

At first it was thought that six buyers would pay the going

price of $305,000 and divide the land among themselves. But no agreement could be reached on specific parcels or prices to be paid. It was soon realized that a single entity would have to acquire the land.

Kenneth Bergen, founder and leader of the organization that was formed to deal with this problem, describes the next step as follows: "Thereupon, The Rural Land Foundation was organized as a non-profit trust. The organization was made non-profit, rather than profit-making, to avoid any conflict between those wishing as much conservation land as possible and those wishing a larger number of saleable lots. The decision to eliminate any profit for the backers was made only after a lively philosophical discussion as to whether the profit motive would be inconsistent with the basic conservation purpose. With a non-profit organization, there is no doubt that more and better land has been set aside for conservation than otherwise would have been the case."[1]

Right from the start the Rural Land Foundation was empowered to buy and sell land as well as hold it for conservation purposes. Organized as a charitable trust, it was funded with contributions of one dollar from each of its eight founding trustees. To this date, after eight land ventures involving $1.6 million and the saving of 155 acres, this is the only money that has actually been contributed to the Rural Land Foundation.

Favoring the land sensitive intentions of its fellow citizens, the Wheeler family sold their land to the Rural Land Foundation for $285,000. According to Ken Bergen: "The purchase was financed by a loan of $199,500 from a local savings bank secured by a first mortgage on the land and two farmhouses, a $50,000 purchase money loan secured by a second mortgage, and a loan of $35,000 from the State Street Bank and Trust Company. The real secret to the success of the financing effort was the credit given by the State Street Bank which was willing to make loans to the Rural Land Foundation on the basis of separate $10,000 guarantees of 30 public spirited Lincoln citizens."[2] It was in fact the credit of the State Street Bank that enabled the Rural Land Foundation to retain the services of Max Mason, a Lincoln landscape architect, and start the process of planning for the land. The accepted plan subdivided the land into eleven lots ranging in size from two to seven acres, a single 1,700-foot curved road with underground utilities, and 54 acres, including most open fields and the old colonial road, to be protected as public open space.

As it turned out the two farmhouses and nine acres of land restricted from further development were sold for $105,000. Eight of the other nine lots were sold at prices ranging from $25,000 to $45,000. Ahead of the game by some $40,000 at this point, the Rural Land Foundation added the last lot to the acreage to be protected and gave 56 acres to the Lincoln Land Conservation Trust for its care and management. After three and a half years of hard work and worry, the Rural Land Foundation celebrated its Wheeler venture with the return of all personal guarantees. As a result of its initial success the Rural Land Foundation was called on to undertake other projects before long.

So it was that early in Lincoln's conservation efforts a second viable option to sprawl was developed. It was really a third option, because gifts of land to the town or other charitable agencies were already a well-established tradition in Lincoln, with the Lincoln Land Conservation Trust created in 1958 leading the way in soliciting gifts of land from those who were in a position to benefit from making such gifts.

Even before the land trust had been formed, the town's open space character had been served by several large gifts of land. Well before gifting was recognized as an important estate planning device, several hundred acres were protected by such individuals as John Pierce, Mary Hathaway, and Julian DeCordova for the sheer love of their land and community. It was their own personal sense of stewardship that saved those acres. It's quite likely that Lincoln's land use ethic might never have developed as it has if it weren't for those early examples. Although on a smaller personal scale, the generous risk taking of the Rural Land Foundation guarantors stands in this tradition. I am quite sure that in several cases the generosity of the guarantors has at least matched that of the early donors because of the limited ability of their families to sustain the potential losses being risked. Although I have never been a guarantor, I get angry when people suggest that our Rural Land Foundation approach is suitable only to rich communities. Sure it takes a little capital to participate in such an endeavor. But it doesn't take that much.

Although no acquisitions were completed in 1967, work proceeded on two acquisitions that resulted in the 1968 purchase of two parcels totaling 70 acres at a gross cost of $187,000, for which reimbursements of $133,000 were obtained. Some of the land purchased was and continues to be in active agriculture while much of the balance is rolling woodland on the banks of the town's reservoir. In addition to these two acquisitions, the commission received two gifts on behalf of the town totaling over five acres.

By the end of 1968 the Conservation Commission had acquired 263 acres since its first purchase in 1960, the Rural Land Foundation was well on its way to protecting the essential natural attributes of the Wheeler Farm, and the Lincoln Land Conservation Trust had completed the protection of an additional 70 acres. Although development was proceeding apace on a two-acre lot basis with some clustering taking place, there was a sense emerging that the town would be able to cope with the waves of change that were clearly upon it. A growing confidence in our community's ability to shape effective responses to the threat of sprawl held us together in the face of mounting pressure. Even as 1968 began it was clear that citizens would need all the courage they could muster to deal with the events that were about to unfold.

In late 1967 the last of the Codman line, Dorothy Codman, passed away, leaving her great house and 15 acres to the Society for the Preservation of New England Antiquities, 25 acres to the Lincoln Land Conservation Trust, and 200 acres to be disposed of by her trustees with the proceeds to be managed for the benefit of Lincoln residents. As generous as this was, it meant that 200 acres of Lincoln's best and most beautiful farm- land, much of it designated for protection in the By-70 plan, was to be offered for sale.

The Planning Board and selectmen responded quickly to the news of this disposition by informing Miss Codman's trustees of the town's wish to acquire, at fair market value, control of the whole parcel. Favoring the protection of the property through use, the Planning Board issued an invitation to ar- chitects and planners for suggestions to include some well- placed single family houses, some moderate-income housing, and some conservation and recreation use. As first steps, the Planning Board then commissioned a soil study of the land along with aerial photographs to provide accurate contour maps. This was a rather brave move on the part of the Planning Board since I still don't know how they were expecting to finance the plans to be selected. Fortunately, unexpected events took over to provide a happy ending.

While contemplating its role in the resolution of the Codman property along with other large parcels expected to be placed on the market soon, the Conservation Commission had already ended one of its long meetings in the late fall of 1968 when one of its members mentioned that the state's Department of Natu- ral Resources was about to lose $1 million in available federal funds for lack of a project to support. Although it was late, the meeting was quickly reconvened and plans set in motion that would result in the acquisition of 570 acres, including 122 acres of the Codman property, for $1.8 million in March of 1969. Known as the Mt. Misery acquisition, this purchase included a broad sweep of open fields in active agriculture, two hills, including one overlooking Walden Pond, and rolling woods. By the time the last purchases were negotiated and all reimburse- ments received, the net cost to the taxpayers of Lincoln was $490,000 plus the interest required to service the borrowings over a twelve-year period. Of the $1.3 million received in reimbursements, $880,000 came from the Bureau of Outdoor Recreation's Land and Water Conservation Fund and $430,000 came from the Massachusetts Self-Help Fund. To be sure, what became possible for Lincoln in this important instance was fortuitous and cannot be put forth as a model for others to follow, except to the extent that determination often leads to unexpected opportunities which must be boldly seized as they appear.

In any case, the financial impact of the Mt. Misery acquisition on the taxpayers of Lincoln worked out pretty much as predicted at the 1969 Town Meeting that overwhelmingly voted its approval. With interest costs, the average net impact of the purchase on the town's tax levy was close to $60,000. An earlier revaluation had raised the town assessments to $45 million so that each dollar in the property tax rate raised $45,000. Dividing the $45 million assessed valuation into the town's 1,200 dwellings indicated an average valuation of close to $40,000. Based on the average $60,000 required to finance the town's share of the purchase over twelve years, it can be said that the Mt. Misery acquisition has cost the average family in town roughly $50 per year for twelve years.

At the time of the acquisition it was understood that development would have resulted in an additional 250 houses that could be expected to fall from $500 to $1,000 short of paying their way. Although this represented a total shortfall of $125,000 to $250,000 per year, an amount substantially in excess of the town's cost of acquisition, the argument was not made on the floor of Town Meeting. Since the building of these houses was only a speculation, the purchase was recommended on the basis of its conservation values and the probable tax impacts of purchasing the land.

As I recall them, the real arguments pro and con on the floor of Town Meeting were not financial. They had more to do with preserving a large piece of Lincoln's most beautiful land for passive recreational use on a regional basis. Although some were concerned about cost, more were concerned about the possible loss of control over this land to state and federal governments that might decide on unwanted facilities or other uses. In short a major issue was local control. Some actually wanted Lincoln to acquire the land with no state and federal assistance. Fortunately we were able to convince most of those at the meeting that the state and federal funding terms expressed in a land use memorandum were clear on the point of continued local control so long as there was no evidence of discrimination between local residents and out-of-towners when it came to permitted uses. Since it was the sense of the town that Lincoln should play a regional open space role, this argument was overcome. More convincing was the contrary argument that with funding support from state and federal conservation agencies, the town would be better protected from intrusion by major state and federal facilities. This indeed turned out to be the case when, shortly after the Mt. Misery acquisition, the state's Department of Public Works (DPW) attempted to run an eight-lane highway along Walden Pond and through the heart of the Mt. Misery acquisition. I believe that the state DPW tabled that plan when they learned that we had acquired land for conservation purposes either side of the fifty-foot road to be widened. Changes in state administration and an end to perceived needs for bigger and better roads since that time have pretty well ended that threat. What is left is a plan to relocate Route 126, now running right along Walden Pond, so that it will cease to intrude on Thoreau's pond. Having acquired much of the land over which the relocated road will run, Lincoln is in a position to facilitate the relocation and hasten the day when Walden Pond will be appropriately restored as a living reminder of Thoreau's stay along its shore.

Although the town's other acquisitions during the 1960s may have been less dramatic than the Mt. Misery acquisition, they were nonetheless of equal importance because they helped to complete the pattern of open space that is now seen as vital to the town's long-term interests. Taken as a whole, the acquisitions of the 1960s protected over 800 acres at a gross cost of

$2.25 million. After reimbursements the town's portion turned out to be close to $600,000, plus interest. The loans, now almost repaid, added between $50 and $100 to the annual property taxes of the average Lincoln resident. I have never heard anyone complain about the financial burdens of these acquisitions although there have been some complaints about seasonal abuse or overuse of several of our conservation areas. The complaints have centered around parking and traffic congestion along with trespassing on private land, especially by cross-country skiers who stray from marked trails. So far these complaints involve problems that can be managed by better surveillance, more clearly marked trails, and strategically located parking areas. A three-man summer ranger program has already gone a long way toward resolving these problems.

Large as it was, the Mt. Misery acquisition did not deal with all the land coming to market in 1969. With the passing of its family patriarch, the Winchell family had to dispose of 186 acres of rolling woodland and farm fields that fronted on both Farrar Road and the Sudbury River. In addition there were still 71 acres of Codman land to be considered. The town clearly had its fill of acquisitions for a while and there was a growing sense of the need for alternatives to two-acre zoning. More creative development would address special housing needs while permitting owners to realize the full and fair value implicit in the town's two-acre zoning. As 1969 drew to a close it was clear that the vision of the By-70 plan was no longer adequate. Although many of its goals had been achieved, the town's land use future had not been fully settled. There were still a lot of privately owned undeveloped land in town and a lot of unmet human needs. To try and bring these together, in January 1970, the selectmen and Planning Board convened a townwide conference to launch a new and more detailed look into Lincoln's education and land use futures, with each to be considered on successive Saturdays. The second Saturday also dealt with town government.

By now the community was focused on the land and, after

participation by over 400 people in the two-day conference, 150 people were willing to sustain their involvement in follow-up committee activities to explore the many aspects of land use in Lincoln. The idea was more than simply coming up with published proceedings of the public meetings or producing a final By-80 report. The idea was to create an ongoing planning presence that would make sure the official town boards didn't get bogged down in day-to-day details. Although the work of these committees was finally pulled together in a final report in 1976, and its findings incorporated in official town planning and activities, there is still a By-80 focus around in the presence of an informed electorate that keeps a close watch on its elected and appointed officials.

The land use portion of the By-80 conference was opened by Professor John C. Keane of the Department of City and Regional Planning at the University of Pennsylvania, who was invited because of his experience with the Brandywine project in Pennsylvania. His talk had considerable influence in shaping our response to Lincoln's growth pressures. His concluding statement rings just as true today as it did in January 1970: "If, as I suspect, your objective will rely heavily on conservation and on preservation and development of useful open space, it's essential for legal reasons that you develop the scientific background, the scientific underpinnings on which you want to base these regulations . . . You need to undertake the studies of existing water quality, studies of soil types, topography, suitability of different types of lands for different types of development. If you are interested in doing this, you need to proceed from a sound scientific basis and then develop your sound economic and legal and social policies consistent with the natural base on which you are building."

Professor Keane's call for a detailed understanding of the Lincoln landscape led to the town's selection by the USDA Soil Conservation Service for a pilot natural resources inventory to be conducted under the leadership of Professor Benjamin Isgur of the University of Massachusetts. The most lasting contribution of this effort was a detailed soil survey with maps showing Lincoln's underlying geology and soil conditions. Delineating the town wetlands, shallow and impermeable soils, rock outcropping, and steep slopes, the resultant maps showed where development could and could not take place if the town were to remain in balance with its natural systems. With this third dimension, we had the base data required to test our zoning ordinances and the arbitrary pressures they placed on Lincoln's varied soils.

The By-80 conference and its follow-up efforts also revealed a strong base of citizen support for appropriate housing for people of low and moderate incomes as well as housing for families with few or no children. For the first time the rezoning of residential land for multiple-family housing on greater than two-acre density became a political possibility. Like major land purchases requiring town bonding, zoning changes in Lincoln require a two-thirds vote at Town Meeting. Although further study was deemed necessary to identify growth constraints in which the limiting factor was the town's water supply, it was estimated that tripling of population to 15,000 could be supported. Out of this conference came a feeling of confidence that the town could relax its defensive development posture and move on to the task of shaping its settlement future.

Armed with the conference's consensus that the town was prepared to consider density development to meet special needs while protecting natural systems, the Planning Board solicited and obtained the Winchell family's willingness to hold off development until a new zoning option was formulated. In addition the Rural Land Foundation was prevailed upon to acquire and hold for $275,000 the 71 remaining Codman acres while special committees explored the feasibility of converting 15 to 20 acres of the Codman land into multiple-family housing and four acres zoned for commercial use into an improved commercial center, while protecting the remaining 45 acres for continued agricultural use. In both cases zoning was used to foster developments that met multiple needs at no cost to the town.

The ultimate success of both ventures established the viability of Lincoln's creative approach.

Having obtained the Winchells' consent to wait, the Planning Board retained the services of three professionals to study and suggest density zoning provisions with sufficient incentive to encourage owners of large tracts to participate in carefully planned developments. After much deliberation and public consideration the town adopted two density zoning provisions. The first, intended initially for the Winchell property, was labeled Open Space Residential District, or OSRD was approved in March, 1971. In brief it enabled owners of parcels of 25 or more acres to subdivide their land into twice the number of units that could be built under the town's two-acre bylaw, provided in essence that 70 percent of the land was protected as open space. The plan was subject to careful environmental impact analysis, and Town Meeting voted its approval by a needed two-thirds majority.

The second density zoning provision, intended for the Codman property, permitted even greater density along the same approval lines, provided 50 percent of the dwelling units qualified as low- and moderate-income housing. It was approved at the March, 1972, Town Meeting. In both cases the town was assured by the two-thirds approval requirements that density developments would not take place without careful scrutiny and substantial townwide support.

At the 1972 meeting the town also voted to relax its two-acre zoning to allow apartments to be built in 10 percent of Lincoln's existing houses through a process of petition to the Zoning Board of Appeals. It was felt that in this way still more families could be accommodated without increased pressure on valued open space. Moreover this seemed a likely way to ease entry into the town for young couples and people of modest means while helping existing residents support and maintain houses that otherwise would have become too large to manage.

As the new density zoning provisions were accepted, planning began on both the Winchell and Codman pieces, the latter having been purchased by the Rural Land Foundation. Since the Planning Board lacked experience with the new condominium zoning provision, it prevailed upon the Winchells to limit their subdivision application to 100 acres, with the rest to be planned after the town had had a chance to study the results of their first effort.

This led to a determination that the 100-acre piece valued at $500,000 could accommodate 40 single-family houses on a two-acre basis. Although the two-acre development plan was intended merely to determine density potential and land value, it clearly revealed the environmental conflicts that would have arisen had the old two-acre system been followed. Houses would have encroached on an otherwise quiet natural pond and houses and roads would have covered productive cropland and sprawled over lovely woods containing deep kettleholes and fragile flora and fauna including lady slippers. The long-used trail system that enabled people to move over the land and around the pond would have been fully blocked. Under the new zoning the plan that resulted in Farrar Pond Village provided for three clusters of 80 townhouse condominiums carefully sited in three clusters on less than 24 acres of land so that important trees and natural features were protected. Leading into the clusters was only one short access road to be owned and maintained by the condominium association, instead of a network of town-owned roads to service two-acre lots. Common septic systems were located well away from the pond so that eutrophication would not be increased. In these and many other ways the density plan resolved the development conflicts posed by a two-acre subdivision while providing twice the number of dwelling units.

As was later demonstrated when its sister project was being considered in 1978, Farrar Pond Village did not encumber the land with more building coverage or more people than a two-acre single family development would have done, nor did it generate more traffic for neighborhood roads. Moreover it resulted in one-fifth the road pavement. Also, since the condominiums attracted so-called empty-nesters or families without children in school, the development was found to be a net contributor to the cost of running the town. Calculations before project approval had estimated a net contribution per dwelling unit of $1,000, or $80,000 for the planned units, as compared with a $40,000 annual shortfall to be expected from new single-family houses. As it turned out, the 80 condominiums of Farrar Pond Village make a net annual contribution of $160,000. Based on these calculations, a careful presentation of the proposed condominium development, and the expressed support of all town boards, the Farrar Pond Village development was approved at the June 1972 special Town Meeting over the opposition of some neighbors who felt the Winchells should leave their land undeveloped and others who feared a serious increase in traffic on neighborhood roads. There was also a feeling expressed that the condominium owners would somehow be different from the rest of their neighbors. In any case, the project was approved and built, the Winchells received $500,000 from the developer, 80 new families moved to Lincoln, and over 70 acres of open space were protected at no public cost.

Although it took several years to really sink in, the implications of Lincoln's Open Space Residential District zoning provision were enormous. Besides providing needed housing for a certain sector of our metropolitan region, it enabled the town and owners of large parcels to work together in packaging land for newcomers in such a way that they would be welcome additions to the community. I say welcome because they do not encroach on natural resources valued by all. In fact they protect them at no cost to the town. They add diversity to the town's social make-up, and they make a net financial contribution to the town that enables other things to happen.

One of those other things was Lincoln Woods, the low- and moderate-income subdivision made possible by the town's second density zoning provision. You'll recall that the Rural Land Foundation had been prevailed upon to acquire and hold 71 acres of Codman land for $275,000 while the town prepared an appropriate settlement format, found a developer and needed state financing, and rezoned the 67 acres of the Codman land which was still in two-acre residential use. While the housing was being considered, the four acres zoned for commercial use were retained by the Rural Land Foundation for later disposition. By July 1972 the town had completed all these steps and appointed a design review committee to work with the selected architectural firm in preparing a plan acceptable to the town. Although the original design was for 150 units, of which 75 would be offered at market prices and the balance subsidized— half for low-income families and the other half for low- and moderate-income families—the design review process led to a final design of 125 units to be located on 12 acres. To make this density compatible with an unsewered town, the project included a package treatment plant to be sited on the corner of the 20-acre farm field to be preserved as a result of the development.

Since the alteration of some wetlands was involved and the development was located in the same watershed as the town well, which complements the town reservoir, careful hydrologic studies were conducted and reviewed in public hearings by the Conservation Commission. Finally, before presenting the plan to the town for a vote, an economic study was made of the proposed development to determine its probable impact on the tax rate. Based on expected school and other municipal costs, and the taxes to be paid by the project, it was estimated that it might fall $80,000 short of paying its way. At last the proposal was put to a vote at the June 1972 special Town Meeting where it passed with the necessary two-thirds vote despite some objection to the number of units and their probable visual impact on Lincoln's small commercial center. Later the 46 acres that were not included in the development were deeded over to the town for conservation purposes.

After more than the usual construction problems, which have since resulted in serious litigation, Lincoln Woods stands fully occupied with the residents very much a part of Lincoln

life. The average land purchase cost per unit was less than
$2,000. The 20-acre farm field in the woods behind the new
community is actively farmed by Codman Community Farms
under the supervision of the Conservation Commission.

Codman Community Farms is a citizen-managed organization that was started with support from the Codman Trust
established by Dorothy Codman with the funds raised from the
sale of land. Now profitable, it retains its own farmer, hires local
youths, owns considerable equipment, occupies the renovated
Codman barns acquired by the town under a separate transac-
tion as a recreation center, and farms over 100 acres of land in
Lincoln, including 40 acres of town-owned land. One of its
major programs is the provision of 160 garden plots available
to Lincoln residents as well as nonresidents.

Taking Farrar Pond Village and Lincoln Woods together,
one can see that Lincoln's new zoning provisions enabled the
conversion of 167 acres into residential and public use in such
a way that dwelling units for 205 families were created. Overall
these more than pay their way, protect at no cost to the town
the valuable natural resources that would otherwise have been
overwhelmed, and add needed diversity to Lincoln's housing
mix.

That in a nutshell is creative development. Considering its
attributes one day prior to giving a talk on the Lincoln experience prompted me to hypothesize that growth is OK if—if it
pays its own way; if it doesn't impair vital natural systems; and
if it helps balance development needs. Later, as I further dis-
tilled my thoughts on the subject, it occurred to me that growth
should pay for the protection of the natural systems that it
threatens and that it too will need. Lincoln's two density zoning options have gone a long way toward proving these two hypotheses.

To finish the Codman story, the Rural Land Foundation
went on to consider the real commercial needs of Lincoln and
interviewed potential developers. Their goal was not to attract
random businesses that would compete in Lincoln for regional

services and supplies already adequately supplied in Boston, Waltham, or other area shopping centers. Right off the goal was to rationalize the town's small commercial center abutting the Codman land and make it attractive for commercial activities appropriate to our local setting. In other words, the idea was to retrieve the money tied up in the land by the Rural Land Foundation through commercial development of appropriate scale. Details included revisions to a busy road, the provision of improved commuter and shopper parking, and the provision of facilities needed by the area's increasing population—a supermarket, bank, and hardware store. Miscellaneous other shops and service facilities, including a relocated post office, completed the development.

Thanks to the serious involvement of dedicated citizens expert in the law and real estate, the Rural Land Foundation managed to attract a superior developer willing to construct under long-term lease what is now known as the Lincoln Mall. The developer worked closely with the Planning Board, and the result was an attractive functional shopping center, well suited to Lincoln's needs, that pays $9,000 a year in rents to the Rural Land Foundation. At specified times in the lease period the Rural Land Foundation has the option to acquire the mall buildings on a sliding-scale purchase basis. Someday the town of Lincoln will own its shopping center. Think of it. Think of it in terms of the potential power of caring citizens who want to have a say in shaping the future of their community.

Although the mapping of Lincoln's soils by the Soil Conservation Service made many of us aware that a lot of undeveloped land in Lincoln was unsuited for development, I believe it is fair to say that these maps as such have never had much impact on Lincoln land use decisions. It wasn't until the Conservation Commission settled on the idea of mapping wetlands and other lands of conservation interest on 200-foot scale topographic maps and combined these with property lines and ownerships on the same maps that we found ourselves in a position to really judge and influence the likely future of Lincoln land use on a plot-by-plot basis. To be sure the soil maps, along with copies of the state's aerial photographs of Lincoln, were helpful in preparing the Conservation Commission's maps, but it was really the two-year interpretive analysis and field work of conservation commissioner Lydia Dane, geologist Leona Champeny, and their many volunteer helpers that resulted in a detailed mapping. In December 1973 this led to the wetland zoning of over 1,200 acres of Lincoln wetlands owned by close to 600 families. To me this effort alone, achieved at a cost of something like $1,200, went a long way toward assuring the future viability of Lincoln's residual rural character. It means fewer failing septic systems and less chance of need for comprehensive sewerage. It protects natural drainage and diminishes the possibility of surface and groundwater pollution.

It should be noted that Lincoln's wetland zoning, like the state's wetland protection laws, does not prohibit all use of wetlands. The town's zoning bylaw created an overlay district where construction of structures is severely limited, subject to Board of Appeals consideration. The state's regulations mandate a public hearing process for the consideration of all proposed wetland alterations and grant conservation commissions broad discretion to impose engineering and construction conditions that assure protection of water flows, quality and quantity. Although local commissions have the power to prohibit certain alterations, all of their determinations are subject to state review and appeal. To many of us the chief contribution of Lincoln's wetland mapping and zoning efforts is the full disclosure of wet areas in the town. No longer can land buyers claim surprise to find portions of their land unsuited to development in seeking relief before the Planning Board and Zoning Board of Appeals. Developers and town officials, including the building inspector, are all on notice as to where wetland limitations must be considered. Looking back over the five years since enactment of Lincoln's wetland zoning, one notes with interest that numerous alterations have taken place in accordance with established proceedings without one denial. Most of the alterations have been for the establishment of driveways or the creation of ponds. I feel safe in saying that, in almost all cases, those proposing the alteration feel they have been helped in the process by the town's free expert advice.

With the wetlands mapped and zoned, the Conservation Commission launched its most ambitious planning project, the survey at 200-foot scale of all the remaining undeveloped land in Lincoln in order to determine and map the remaining Land of Conservation Interest—a term we coined—that needed special treatment before its development. Fortunately the commission had several senior native members who were intimately familiar with the Lincoln landscape. One of these, J. Quincy Adams, is a retired architect with a deep commitment to rational land use in Lincoln. Quincy is a direct descendant of the presidents; his love of the land must stem from his grandfather, Charles Francis Adams, who moved from Quincy, Massachusetts, and settled in Lincoln in 1894. It is this man who was active in the creation of Boston's Metropolitan District Commission and chaired it while Frederic Law Olmstead planned Boston's emerald necklace of metropolitan green spaces. Active on the Conservation Commission since its inception in 1958, Quincy now dedicated himself fully to the architecture and implementation of a new open space plan for Lincoln.

Before launching himself into a detailed study of Lincoln's twenty-three 200-foot scale maps to identify Land of Conservation Interest, Quincy challenged us to develop objective criteria that could be applied with reasonable confidence. The goal was to identify the land that should be saved regardless of Lincoln's future population. After much deliberation we settled on the following five criteria:

1. Place in Lincoln Conservation Plan: Its position and importance within the overall concept, its area, its relationship to conservation areas of neighboring communities;

2. Quality and accessibility of land for public use, under Conservation Commission criteria for public use, including trail easements;

3. Productivity of land for farm and forestry products;

4. Visual aspects; open space adjacent to public ways and public areas, as part of the trail connector pattern;

5. Wetlands and watershed as storage areas and protection for public water supplies.

By this time the town's twenty-three base maps already reflected lands permanently protected by the Conservation Commission and land trust in green crayon. The wetlands were all marked with yellow crayon. Land protected under permanent conservation restriction or owned by semipublic institutions such as Massachusetts Audubon and not subject to public control were crayoned in dark green with black stripes. These clearly delineated the parts of Lincoln's open space puzzle that were already protected in some permanent fashion.

Once we all agreed on criteria, Quincy proceeded to study the twenty-three 200-foot scale maps and insisted that the commission review with him each map as it neared completion. On this scale map each inch square covers 40,000 square feet, or a builder's acre. So you can see that we worked at a pretty fine level of detail. In this way Quincy assured that the final plan would be the commission's plan, one we would all strongly support because it incorporated all of our special interests, including farmland, trails, and special views.

When Quincy was done, in early 1975, we were surprised to learn that Lincoln's Land of Conservation Interest totaled 1,453 acres and was held by 101 owners in 119 parcels. The 200-foot scale maps were then photographed and reduced to a 1,000-foot scale in color.

As the Conservation Commission proceeded with the careful preparation of its ultimate open space plan, two events occurred to accelerate the effort. First, under a new administration, the state moved to change a decision of long standing regarding the relocation of a major highway dissecting Lincoln and its open spaces. There is no need for details; it had long been decided that Route 2, as it goes through Lincoln, was to be relocated toward the northern edge of the town and along the new Minuteman National Park which extends from the Old North Bridge in Concord, along the April 19, 1975, battle route in Lincoln to the town green in Lexington, so that the road presently going through the park could be closed to through traffic. Since the additional load to be carried by the presently overburdened Route 2 could not be carried without major alteration that would severely impact the existing corridor at a cost higher than the relocation, it had long been expected that a new alignment would result that would allow recycling of the existing road into a town road; it was intended as a major regional access to Lincoln's evolving pattern of open spaces. Completion of the open space plan had to be hastened for use in the Route 2 environmental impact process.

Equally imperative was a decision by the town assessors that Lincoln would respond promptly to the state's mandate for 100 percent valuations by 1980, and that undeveloped land which had long been assessed at nominal values would be appraised on the basis of its full development potential. When it was learned from the assessors that initial calculations showed undeveloped land in Lincoln would rise in assessed valuation from $1 million to $11 million and that its tax burden would rise from $67,000 to $275,000 per year, it was clear that a lot of undeveloped land would be forced on the market that otherwise would have been sold at an orderly rate over a prolonged period. Lincoln had to prepare at once for the sudden conversion of all its remaining undeveloped land. Clearly we had to move.

To many the projected increase in land taxes was not perceived as a destabilizing factor. After all, assessments of the rest of the town were to be raised from $50 million to $120 million and would still pay taxes of $3 million. Surely a reduction in taxes of $200,000 on developed property was only fair. Hadn't the large landowners been getting a free ride? Well, to the extent that the proposed revaluations reflected proved development potential based on subdivision plans and proved percolation tests, the probable marketing duration, and costs involved with converting land to other uses, it would be fair. The trouble was that, as initially proposed, these factors were not fully taken into consideration. Finally they were. Moreover the shift to 100 percent valuation altered the economics of holding undeveloped land in Lincoln. I well remember talking with a trustee who represented the ownership interests of a substantial parcel of undeveloped land. In brief he said that as long as the land appreciated at 10 percent a year and paid negligible taxes it was better to hold it than sell it, pay taxes, and invest the money elsewhere. Once property taxes reached 3 percent of land value two things happened to change that. First, there was insufficient cash flow to pay the taxes, so his trust was confronted with piecemeal liquidation and, second, other investments offered a better return. In sum he was telling me that the delicate balance that justified his retention of the land as a trustee was in jeopardy. Obviously a lot of other landowners were coming to the same conclusion.

According to the town's assessors Lincoln's privately owned land then in, or available for, residential use was owned as 1,605 parcels in lot sizes as follows:

Lot size in acres	Number of parcels	Total acreage
0–1	349	230
1–2	581	863
2–3	278	638
3–5	181	682
5–10	116	806
10–25	65	962
over 25	35	1,677
	1,605	5,858

Since achievement of the commission's conservation objectives for each parcel designated as Land of Conservation Interest did not necessarily mean no development, it could be seen that the commission's plan left considerable room for future growth. As a matter of fact, to the extent that conservation goals could be achieved through density development, as was done in the cases of Farrar Pond Village and Lincoln Woods, it could be argued that the plan provided for more dwelling units than the town would be likely to allow in the absence of careful planning. In any case the task of the commission was now clear. It was to develop a plan that took into account the special circumstances of each of the 119 parcels of conservation interest, and each of their 101 owners, and was satisfactory to the town. This meant the establishment of a communications process with each owner to work out a mutually desirable future for each parcel of land of conservation interest. This was to be done first by a special letter introducing the finished plan, and by direct communication with each of these landowners as part of the implementation phase. To quantify in dollar terms the task to be done, the commission retained the services of a leading Boston appraiser to estimate the value of the land designated for special attention. In the course of two days he was able to estimate the value of Lincoln's land of conservation interest at $7.5 million. At this point we were able to report that Lincoln had a $7.5 million open space problem covering 1,453 acres held in 119 parcels by 101 ownership interests. The question was how to deal with this problem in the most creative way and at minimum cost to the town.

Knowing each piece of land of conservation interest by owner, development potential, and probable value, we discussed the circumstances of each in order to develop a preferred strategy for achieving needed protection. In many cases it was clear that purchase was the only answer; in others the features that interested us could be saved in the subdivision process. This was particularly true where trail connectors were the principal interest. In the case of farmland, we made sure that each owner was well aware of opportunities under the state's preferential farmland assessment program, and we studied each parcel to see if careful development was compatible with protection of the actual farmland. Aware that the commonwealth was preparing a development rights acquisition program, we made a real effort to qualify farmland under the state's preferential program which includes a sixty-day right-of-first-refusal prior to a sale that would remove land from agricultural use. In other cases we saw opportunity to solicit gifts of land or the establishment of conservation restrictions. By the time we were ready to incorporate our findings in a report to be published, we had concluded that protection of Lincoln's remaining privately owned and controlled natural systems would require an expenditure of $4.5 million and that after reimbursement, estimated at 50 percent, it would impact Lincoln taxes as shown in table 1. As shown in this table, the estimated annual fiscal impact of the proposed open space plan would have started at $118,000 in 1977/78, built to a peak of $231,000 in 1980/81, and then eased until it disappeared in the year 2000. Compared to Lincoln's 1976 tax levy of $3.2 million this represented an increase of 3.7 percent to a maximum impact of 7.2 percent. To the extent that there were no offsetting savings, a family paying taxes of $1,500 could expect the program to raise its taxes by $56 to $108 per year. With these numbers it became a matter of town priority whether or not to support the program. A vote of endorsement to be called for at Town Meeting would reveal the extent of voter support.

As the impact of 100 percent valuations became apparent to Lincoln landowners, a rush to sell became a distinct possibility just as the open space plan was nearing completion. In order to give the town and landowners a reasonable chance to respond to the new valuations, the assessors were prevailed upon to delay their implementation by one year. Prior to this extension the Conservation Commission printed 5,000 copies of its 1,000-foot scale Open Space Map and sent it to all Lincoln residents along with an introductory cover letter that stressed the availability of several landowner options in dealing with land of conservation interest. These options would later be

TABLE I

Annual Fiscal Impact of Proposed $4.5 Million in Land Acquisitions
with Initial 2-Year Funding, 50% Reimbursements, and 20-Year Residual Bonding at 5%

(all figures in $000)

	1977/78	1978/79	1979/80	1980/81	1981/82	1982/83	1983/84	1984/85	1999/2000
Annual Acquisitions	$1,500	$1,500	$750	$750	$—	$—	$—	$—	—
Short-Term Funding									
Min. Appropriation 3%	45	45	23	23					
Annual 2-year borrowing	1,455	1,455	727	727					
Cumulative 2-year borrowing	1,455	2,910	2,182	1,454					
Reimbursements at 50% and 2-Year Lag			750	750	375	375			
Long-Term Bonding—20 years—as amortized									
1978/79 Acquisitions			705	670	635	600	565	530	
1979/80 Acquisitions				705	670	635	600	565	
1980/81 Acquisitions					341	315	289	263	
1981/82 Acquisitions						341	315	289	
Principal Payments									
1978/79 Acquisitions			35	35	35	35	35	35	
1979/80 Acquisitions				35	35	35	35	35	
1980/81 Acquisitions					26	26	26	26	
1981/82 Acquisitions						26	26	26	
Total Annual Principal Payments			35	70	96	122	122	122	
Cumulative Long-Term Bonding	—	—	670	1,305	1,550	1,769	1,647	1,525	—
Total Cumulative Debt	$1,455	$2,910	$2,852	$2,759	$1,550	$1,769	$1,647	$1,525	—
Interest at 5%	73	145	143	138	107	88	82	76	—
Annual Fiscal Impact (3% appropriations + Interest + Principal)	$118	$190	$201	$231	$203	$210	$204	$198	—
Present Debt Service Obligations									
Conservation	$75	$62	$59	$47	$5	$—	$—	$—	—
Other excluding water bonds	190	159	154	138	120	116	62	60	—
Total	$265	$221	$213	$185	$125	$116	$62	$60	—
Combined Program Impact and Present Debt Service	$383	$411	$414	$416	$328	$326	$266	$258	—

detailed as shown in table 2, which describes several of the ways Lincoln has learned to deal with large pieces of land while providing owners a range of after-tax values close to or higher than those available to them through straight two-acre development. Table 2 shows that by packaging land differently it may be possible to realize development value on an after-tax basis with 10 to 125 dwelling units as well as none at all through public acquisition. In addition the letter stressed the availability of limited and permanent conservation restrictions and preferential farmland assessment that could neutralize the impact of the coming revaluation.

I am convinced that, despite this mailing, the assessors' extension provided the time needed for landowners, town boards, and other citizens to come together and work out a satisfactory future for Lincoln's privately owned undeveloped land. I was vacationing in Florida in late December of 1976 when a telegram telling me of the assessors' decision to extend their implementation deadline arrived. From that time on the pace of land use planning in Lincoln has been at fever pitch.

With the assessors' extension as a spur the commission completed Lincoln's new open space plan in time for public distribution prior to the March Town Meeting. It had been the intention of the commission to request a $3 million bonding authorization to underwrite the cost of its proposed $4.5 million acquisition program, but it soon became evident that the town was not ready to commit itself to such an important program. As a result the commission moved to pass over its endorsement motion, along with two proposed acquisitions, until citizens had a chance to study the new plan and to take up the matter again at a special Town Meeting in June.

Going into the March meeting the Planning Board had become concerned about the impact of 100 percent evaluation on parcels not designated as being land of conservation interest. They were concerned that land of special neighborhood interest, particularly land with sufficient frontage to enable development without subdivision approval, would be sold before neigh-

TABLE 2

For Sale—100-Acre Farm—$500,000 (Includes 30 Acres of Cropland)
Some Possible Futures—Two-Acre Zoning With Density Variations

	Options								
	A	B	C	D	E	F	G	H	I
No. Dwelling Units	50	—	25	15	25	100	125	10	10
No. Acres Urbanized	100	—	50	30	50	30	15	20	20
No. Acres Retained in Agriculture	—	30	0–30	30	15	30	30	30	30
Design Influence									
Town Siting Control	min.	—	min.	large[5]	min.	full	full	large	large
Municipal Cost Profile	none	—	none	large	none	full	full	large	large
Impact on Owner ($000)									
Gross Income	500	500	250	500	500	500	500	350	390
Cost Basis	50	50	25	50	50	50	50	10	30
Taxable Income	450	450	225	450	450	450	450	340	360
Tax @ 35%[1]	157	157	78	157	157	157	157	120	126
Net Gain	293	293	147	293	293	293	293	220	234
Value to Owner									
Net Gain	293	293	147	293	293	293	293	220	234
Tax Basis	50	50	25	50	50	50	50	10	10
Tax Shelter Value[2]	—	—	125	—	—	—	—	200	180[4]
Net Realized by Owner	343	343	297[4]	343	343	343	343	430	424
Impact on Town ($000)									
Land Purchase (50%)	—	250	—	—	125[6]	(100)[7]	—	—	—
Annual Shortfall	75	—	37	—	37	—	100	0–10	0–10
Payout[3]	—	3–4 yrs.	—	—	3–4 yrs.	—	—	—	—

Options

A. Total development.
B. Total town acquisition.
C. Owner develops half—balance given to town or restricted.
D. Rural Land Foundation type self-development.
E. Town purchases half—balance developed by owner.
F. Incentive zoning—Lincoln's Open Space Residential Development (OSRD)
G. Density development for subsidized housing.
H. Combination of D and gift as in C.
I. Purchase of development rights on cropland plus 10 acres of woodlot @ bargain sale price of $1000/acre with 100% state funding. Total gift of balance.

Notes

[1] 25% of first $50,000 gain, plus 35% of balance, plus 9% Massachusetts tax less its federal tax deduction value—all called 35%.
[2] Estimated at 50% of gift value. Would be slightly less if development rights only were given.
[3] Assumes no bonding. If bonded, compare annual debt service to annual shortfall.
[4] Note $250,000 gift at net cost of $46,000 to owner. Could be recouped in increased value of developed lots.
[5] Siting and design control effectively in town hands.
[6] Could be reduced by gifts of abutters to town's share.
[7] Net contribution to cost of municipal services.

[8] Gift comprised of $4,000 × 40 acres = $160,000 plus 40 acres × $5,000 = $200,000 = $360,000.

Special Notes Owner impact figures do not reflect economic value of retained agricultural land. Town impact figures do not reflect economic benefits of protected agricultural cash flows.

borhoods could exercise influence on the future of key parcels. To deal with this the Planning Board established a separate program to identify parcels that might require special treatment. To accomplish this they organized a Neighborhood Lot Program, involving 150 residents from different neighborhoods to study each piece of land not being studied by the commission. By the time of the June meeting it was clear that the Planning Board and Conservation Commission programs had to be dovetailed into one comprehensive program for the town, and funds were requested to complete the studies in an integrated fashion prior to a comprehensive land use conference scheduled for November.

Nevertheless at the June meeting the Conservation Commission requested and received overwhelming support for its published open space plan. Moreover the two acquisitions postponed from the March meeting were easily approved. Together these involved the purchase of 56 acres at a cost of $360,000. State reimbursement and private gifts reduced the town's cost to $245,000. Along with the purchases, gifts of a ten-acre field, and the restriction of two parcels totaling 38 acres resulted in the protection of 100 more acres of the 1,453 designated as being of conservation interest in the open space plan. Clearly Lincoln citizens had confidence in the work of their town boards. The June Town Meeting also voted the funds requested to coordinate the joint Planning Board/Conservation Commission studies. It wouldn't be long before the expression "creative development" as it relates to land conversion would be coined for use in a report entitled "Undeveloped Land In Lincoln, Massachusetts," prepared for the November conference.

Since the March meeting the Planning Board had divided the town into eight broad neighborhoods and recruited 150 people to serve on neighborhood study committees. These committees held neighborhood meetings attended by 500 people, during which each piece of undeveloped land was considered. Owners of pieces of public interest were queried as to future plans for their land. When it was decided to dovetail this effort into the

Conservation Commission's open space plan to come up with one land use plan for the town, it was also decided to work within the framework of the neighborhood study program. By the time the final report was prepared it was learned that there were 3,337 acres of undeveloped land in Lincoln held in 440 parcels. Of these, owners indicated 1,851 acres probably would be developed soon while 1,486 acres probably would not. Of the land to be developed, it looked as though 329 acres were not of special protection interest, 168 acres were of neighborhood interest, and 1,354 of conservation interest. Of those not to be developed, 687 acres were of conservation interest and 799 acres of no protection interest. There was no land of neighborhood interest in this category. A careful study of the configuration of the undeveloped parcels indicated a development potential of 628 new house lots. A second study of development potential based on the town's soil maps showing on-site sewage disposal limitations indicated a development capacity of 817 lots.

For the first time Lincoln had a pretty good sense of its real growth potential under existing zoning. Assuming a maximum number of apartments under the zoning bylaw that permits them in 10 percent of Lincoln's dwellings, and full development of all potential lots with 3.5 persons per household, it could be calculated that Lincoln would peak at a population of 7,400. Assuming development of the probable lots to be sold, the town's population would reach 6,600. These figures presumed no further protection of undeveloped land except through possible clustering within the town's two-acre basic density limitation.

The report went on to show that there were several large parcels of undeveloped land that could be developed on a density basis with town encouragement and approval. Study of these lots showed that their more dense development would increase the maximum and probable population figures to 8,000 and 7,500, respectively. It also showed that density development of some of these parcels was compatible with protection of their portions which are of conservation interest.

In sum the report presented a graph similar to the simplified one that follows, showing conservation objectives that would require acquisition totaling $5.7 million could be achieved for $1.3 million with the full use of creative development.

Since Lincoln's experience proved that creative development could make a substantial net contribution to the cost of town services, it could have been argued that maximum reliance on creative development could actually ease the town's property tax rates on present dwellings. This is such an important point that it bears rereading.

With this report Lincoln residents had a thorough awareness of where future change would have to take place. If there were to be elderly housing, more moderate-income housing, more stores and services, light industry, or other special needs met, it would have to take place on the available blank places in Lincoln's planning maps. If trails were to be salvaged, remaining unprotected farmland saved, or special views protected,

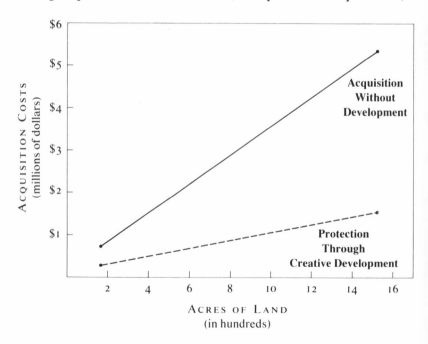

that too was clearly shown on the maps. When the town citizens came together to discuss the future of undeveloped land in Lincoln, they came with a package that included the Undeveloped Land Report and another report providing historical and demographic background which raised the questions to be discussed. The questions dealt with citizen attitudes toward growth, the need for housing for the elderly and people of moderate incomes, more stores and services, future municipal needs, and land to be protected. They had also been given a summary of the responses to a townwide questionnaire on elderly housing needs and interests.

Over 400 people participated in the November 1977 land use conference held in the Lincoln schools. After hearing morning and afternoon speakers, town citizens broke up into twenty groups to discuss the future of Lincoln's undeveloped land. The available materials made it possible to deal at a fine level of detail. It was almost like playing a giant game of Monopoly with fellow citizens.

Out of this came a new endorsement for Lincoln's planning. The work to be done was clear for all to see. Undeveloped land was no longer an indefinite something to be saved from some threatening "them." It was now a resource with which we might meet real town needs while protecting well-defined natural features and systems. Large parcels up for sale and development could be studied in terms of their different needs and opportunities. Town officials could confidently explore and pursue positive approaches to several parcels being considered for development. The Conservation Commission could also pursue with confidence acquisition proposals for large parcels where development was not considered appropriate. Four major initiatives sprang from the November conference.

The first involved the desirability of repeating the Farrar Pond Village experience with a new condominium development. The Winchell family, which had consented in 1969 to withhold 87 of their 187 acres while the town gained experience from their Farrar Pond Village development, were anxious to dispose of their remaining undeveloped land. Their question was whether the town favored 30 single-family houses spread over the land, much of which was designated as land of conservation interest, or 60 townhouse condominiums tightly clustered away from the land the Conservation Commission wanted to see saved. The results of the November conference encouraged the owners and their developer to undertake the costly planning involved in presenting another condominium proposal under Lincoln's Open Space Residential District zoning option.

Second, unrelated owners of four large abutting properties with substantial land of conservation interest were motivated to retain a developer who would plan their land as a single entity under the town's evolving clustering provision in a way that would save most of the land needed to protect the boundaries of Lincoln's historic cemetery at no cost to the town. One small piece was to be bought by the cemetery commission for cemetery purposes.

Third, the Conservation Commission was encouraged to pursue negotiations with a trust that owned 250 acres, almost all of which was designated as land of conservation interest. At the time, it looked as if all the land would be offered for sale. The commission saw its task as determination of the building potential and dollar value of the several pieces comprising the 250 acres, identification of where this development potential was in conflict with features to be protected, and work with the Planning Board in preparing options for achieving conservation goals at minimum cost to the town. As it turned out, only 45 acres along the banks of Sandy Pond became available and those were acquired for $140,000, while six abutting acres were deed-restricted to complete the protection of the northwest shore of the town's 156-acre reservoir.

Finally, although the questionnaire on elderly housing indicated that residents favored dispersed units to a large development, sufficient interest was shown to encourage town boards to investigate actively the possibility of clustering units on a 47-acre piece near the center of the town that was soon to be sold.

Although rooted in the 1977 conference, this effort was not launched until the June 1978 meeting, when the owners offered to hold the land off the market while the town considered its use for elderly and other housing. With a quarter of this piece being open farmland along a major town road, it was important to come up with an option that protected the farmland. Although town purchase of some of this land to achieve its goals was a perceived option, careful study by the commission indicated that the possibility of achieving conservation goals by limited development, financed (it was hoped) by the Rural Land Foundation, preempted the need to spend public funds for this purpose. The best-perceived option was one of creative development to meet specific town needs. Since there were no other large undeveloped parcels conveniently located near the town's shopping area and public transportation, this seemed an important option to pursue. To complicate matters, this parcel is located in the town's well site watershed, making sewage disposal an important issue. Moreover an abutting 37-acre parcel was also being considered for sale by its owners, raising the possibility of another joint development for better flexibility and integration. All these things had to be considered.

Creative development of the sort practiced in Lincoln is not only an imaginative planning process, it is also a sensitive and complex political process. It is one thing for a neighborhood to accept the "inevitable" loss of undeveloped land to conventional development just like everybody else does. It is quite another to participate in the conversion of neighborhood undeveloped land into new forms that satisfy multiple community needs, particularly when increased density or new types of housing are involved. It is hoped that the following careful description of the issues and events that led to Lincoln's second condominium development will provide a sense of the dynamics involved in reaching for highest common denominator land use solutions.

As the proposal for a new condominium development next to Farrar Pond Village began to take shape, much neighborhood opposition surfaced. Families living in single-family housing along the road leading to the proposed development were fearful of increased traffic. There was still resentment that the owners had chosen to develop their property at all. Some felt that the Farrar Pond Village development was enough to ask of the neighborhood. If further development were needed by the owners to raise funds, why not limit it to a few large lots? In any case these neighbors banded together to resist another condominium development.

The residents of the still new Farrar Pond Village also decided to resist the proposed development. Some felt that another such development would reduce the value of their units, which had already shown substantial appreciation. Others were concerned that another condominium development would mean more open space with still more pressure for public use. There were reports of condominium dwellers intimidating hikers and cross-country skiers on the public trails that had been negotiated onto the open portion of Farrar Pond Village when it was approved. The public's right to use these trails apparently had not been sufficiently publicized in the sale of Farrar Pond Village units.

Not all neighborhood sentiment was against another condominium project. The Farrar Pond Association, comprised of the landowners ringing the pond, were strongly in favor of the proposal. They were well aware that density development was the only practical way to protect the pond from visual intrusion and loss of its wilderness aspect.

For its part the Conservation Commission had marked some 40 of the 87 acres as being of conservation interest. Since most of this land overlooked Farrar Pond and the Sudbury River, it represented much of the land's value under low-density development. At this stage of the proceedings it was estimated that the land designated as being of conservation interest represented $400,000 of an overall $600,000 value.

As the condominium proposal came into focus in the winter and early spring of 1978, still another issue that affected the final outcome came into play. For some time Lincoln had been concerned about the adequacy of its water supply. Town officials were aware that tying into the Metropolitan District Commission was rapidly disappearing as a practical option because of existing MDC shortages. The Clean Water Act had raised questions of the long-range suitability of Sandy Pond as Lincoln's main water source because of turbidity and other quality problems which have since been found to be manageable. Preparation of the 1976 open space plan had focused on the vulnerability of the town's Tower Road well site to contamination from existing, let alone further, development in the well site watershed. This had led to a joint Water Board/Conservation Commission effort to study Lincoln's developed water supplies and to explore the town for other potential sources. With much of Lincoln's undeveloped land up for conversion, it soon became clear that this too was an urgent task.

As fate would have it, extensive testing showed few remaining well sites in Lincoln, with the best and most promising located on Winchell property at the edge of Farrar Pond. Because of underlying geology and the configuration of the land, it was determined that protection of the new well site was fully compatible with the proposed condominium development and would be made available to the town at no cost with approval of the development. Failure to approve it would require the expenditure of an estimated $275,000 to purchase the well site, which included much but not all of the land designated as being of conservation interest.

Going into the final hearings prior to Town Meeting, the Winchell proposal called for the development of 58 townhouse condominiums based on a two-acre potential development scheme of 32 lots, one of which already included a house and another to be reserved for future family development. With further nudging and pushing by the Conservation Commission it was apparent that the development would protect the land of conservation interest at no cost to the town. It became apparent in the hearings that the preceding development, Farrar Pond Village, had not yet become integrated into the life of the neighborhood. This was soon to change as the "we's" and "they's" came together to review the proposed development. But this was not to happen until one final outburst on the floor of Town Meeting, where the proposal was rejected in favor of further study and revision prior to possible reconsideration at a special Town Meeting scheduled for the following June to consider that and other land use matters.

Looking back, one can see that the Winchell proposal was first voted down because there were still too many unanswered questions. Although the proposed plan presumed the existence of 32 lots, based on limited testing for septic systems, each of the lots had not been fully tested. The neighbors wanted to know exactly how many units would be built. There was also a question as to the traffic impact to be generated by the double-density condominium project as compared with the likely alternative of a straight two-acre development. Some wanted to see single-family houses so that there would be more school children to bolster Lincoln's sagging school population. Underneath the surface there was a feeling that the proposed rezoning would create a "windfall" for the owners which could serve as a point of negotiation to reduce the proposed density below the two-for-one allowed by the town's density zoning ordinance.

As the discussion proceeded on the floor of the March 1978 Town Meeting, it soon became clear that the project was not ready for approval. Despite its clear financial advantage, Lincoln voters were not prepared to vote against a neighborhood that felt beset by town boards. Despite the acknowledged probability that purchase of the new well site and other land of conservation interest would cost upwards of $400,000, while the proposed zoning would protect these resources at no public cost and would generate an estimated $120,000 in annual net tax contributions above and beyond what could be expected from single-family houses, the town turned down the proposal.

Shortly thereafter the Planning Board went to work to obtain answers to the questions that had been raised at Town Meeting. To do this it enlisted representatives of the "embattled" neighborhood and Farrar Pond Village to form fact-finding task forces. One was assigned the task of developing traffic data that would show whether the proposed development would generate more traffic than the single-family development to which the Winchells were entitled. Another task force undertook a population study to see whether more people would live on the land under one of the two basic possibilities. Still another studied the relative amount of land to be covered by the two proposals. And a fourth looked into design alternatives that might generate equivalent funds for the owners with minimum adverse impact on the neighborhood.

For their part the owners and their developer agreed to cooperate with the task force groups and respond to their questions. Comprehensive test pitting was undertaken to determine the maximum number of dwelling units permitted under the town's two-acre zoning, which in turn would determine the number of townhouse condominiums that might be built. When this was completed the Planning Board retained a professional appraiser to settle the question of what the land was worth under each of three options: straight two-acre development, clustered housing based on two-acre density, and the proposed townhouse condominiums. Although there was still a sense of frustration among some of the neighbors, the information gathered in this process went a long way toward defusing the issues and led to an overwhelming vote of approval at the June meeting.

First it was demonstrated that the land would indeed support 32 single-family houses. Next it was learned that the proposed condominium development did not entail a windfall for the owners, that the land could be sold at a higher value for development as single-family lots. This was a point the owners had made all along; now they were vindicated. Then it was learned through careful traffic counting that single-family houses in new Lincoln subdivisions generated close to twice as many automobile trips per day as did the existing condominiums. It was argued that in the absence of teenage drivers the quality of driving would be safer. As for population, it was learned that single-family dwellings in new Lincoln subdivisions housed twice as many people as did the existing Farrar Pond Village condominiums. Similarly it was learned that the average new house in Lincoln was twice as big as the proposed condominiums. It was already known that the proposed development required only one-fifth the length of road required by two-acre development. Finally, the alternate design task force was unable to come up with a lower-density plan that would achieve the conservation goals of the proposed development while providing equivalent value to the Winchells.

As a result of their work, however, it was learned that slight modification of Lincoln's Open Space Residential District to allow 20 percent of the units to be free-standing instead of the original 15 percent would improve the housing mix by attracting a few more young families with children. By the time the June meeting rolled around the mood of suspicion had shifted to one of acceptance and the proposed subdivision was easily approved.

Although the new development, called Lincoln Ridge, is not yet complete, I suspect that one of its most lasting contributions will be the lowering of barriers between Lincoln Village residents and their single-family home neighbors and a better overall understanding of the land conversion process in Lincoln. No more would land sellers be seen as villains. From now on they would be regarded as part of the creative process by which Lincoln builds a better community.

A second important outcome of the 1977 land use conference was the encouragement of four separate owners of abutting parcels, comprising 74 acres designated as land of conservation interest, to cooperate in the development of their separate pieces on a combined cluster basis so that open fields would be protected along with rolling woodland near the Lincoln Cemetery. In addition cluster development along the lines being considered by the Planning Board would require only one access road and would permit the establishment of vital trail connectors, all at no cost to the town.

There are really only two points I want to make about the process that made this outcome possible. First, the Planning Board saw the possibility of revising the town's cluster bylaw so that clustering was no longer limited to widely detached houses each on a separate acre with common land limited to 50 percent of the site. Town acceptance of Farrar Pond Village had encouraged them to prepare a change to the cluster provision that permitted tight clustering of dwelling units in lily-pad-like clusters floating in a pond of open space. This clustering was really made possible by acceptance of the Farrar Pond Village condominium concept that made close living and management of common areas feasible. Second, active encouragement of the four landowners by town officials provided the incentive necessary for them and their developer to undertake the planning necessary to formulate a viable plan.

I am quite sure that without this support each owner would have proceeded with a separate two-acre subdivision. In this event the Conservation Commission would have had to negotiate with each owner to protect land of conservation interest. This would have meant acquisitions and fewer dwelling units. As matters are working out no dwelling units are being preempted, road-building and site preparation costs are substantially reduced, dwellings are clustered in the best possible locations, and special areas are being protected at no public cost. In fact, only 20 acres carrying 26 dwelling units in seven clusters will be privately owned. The rights of way will contain 2.5 acres, and 51 acres will become conservation land. In addition, as a result of town cooperation, one owner gave 6.5 acres bordering the cemetery to the town and sold another 2.7 acres for possible expansion of the cemetery. Overall a total of 83.5

acres was converted from four separate ownerships into public and private use that make exceptional land use sense.

Another outcome of the November 1976 land use conference was broad understanding and support for the Conservation Commission's negotiations with the trustees of the Sandy Pond Trust, which owned 250 acres of strategically located land in Lincoln. Strategically located, that is, because of their location in the Sandy Pond watershed and their setting in a broad green-belt running along Minuteman National Park in the north, sweeping around Sandy Pond, reaching over Pine Hill to Walden Pond, and stretching out along the Sudbury River to the Federal Wildlife Preserve in Wayland. Many of us feel this whole area should be protected as an Emerson-Thoreau pre-serve to be enjoyed by the public in conjunction with the much smaller Minuteman Park. The Sandy Pond Trust property is one of two major parcels of undeveloped land left to protect in this broad sweep of land. An 87-acre piece behind Walden Pond, owned by the J. Quincy Adams family, is the other major piece needed to complete this vision.

In any case, the advent of 100 percent valuation in early 1977 had prompted the trustees of the Sandy Pond Trust to inform the town that all its land was being considered for sale. Out of courtesy the town was offered first consideration. Working with the selectmen and Finance Committee in negotiating the future of this land, the Conservation Commission launched the negotiations by setting forth a careful process for determining the land developability and its fair market value. Before releas-ing the land for appraisal, a decision was made to retain the services of the town's engineering consultants to prepare a pos-sible subdivision plan for the land, based on its soil capabilities. As it turned out this was the most important step we could have taken. It also marked the first time that we took this step in determining land value. I shudder at the thought of all the acquisitions we had completed without this important step. In any case, we had finally become aware that value was related to developability and that developability was not always apparent from surface conditions.

It is interesting to note that it took three efforts to reach a useful approximation of development potential. The first layouts from the town's consulting engineers were a set of traditional maximum development plans that ignored soil conditions and other development limitations. Knowing that Sandy Pond was a shallow granite basin with most of its till deposited in the southern portion of town, which was widely developable, I was stunned to find myself looking at two-acre and old one-acre lots all over the parcels. When I pointed this out, the consulting engineer replied that he thought we had called for a "maximum development plan."

After being instructed to apply his firm's knowledge of Lincoln's subsurface soil conditions in formulating a possible development scheme, the engineer returned with plans that showed a total of 36 lots. I thought we were getting somewhere. At least I felt that way until I asked him for an estimate of his range of error. When he replied plus-or-minus 20 lots, I was again bewildered. When asked what it would take to narrow the range of error, the consulting engineer replied that careful test pitting of selected areas was needed. Study of the map indicated that 32 sites would have to be tested. He estimated this would be accomplished in four days at a cost of $1,200. Fortunately the Sandy Pond trustees gave us permission to proceed with this work provided we paid for it and shared the results. At last the consulting engineer came up with plans that indicated 36 lots, plus-or-minus four. Knowing where these sites were, we were now in position to judge the land's potential conflicts between development and conservation. We were also in position to charge appraisers with the task of assessing this development potential.

I simply cannot overstate the importance of this step. I am sure that without it we could not have concluded satisfactory negotiations for the 45-acre piece acquired at the special June

1978 Town Meeting. As it turned out, the town voted to purchase this piece for $140,000. The Sandy Pond trustees decided to sell only this parcel in 1978 and decided to hold the remainder indefinitely. To accommodate the town's wish to complete protection of the northwest shore of Sandy Pond through this one acquisition, the trustees agreed, as part of our negotiations, to deed-restrict development on an abutting six acres and to grant an easement over an old cart road that traverses this piece on its way to other old roads that now form paths around the pond.

I hesitate to think what this land would have been deemed to be worth in the absence of its test pitting. I cringe at the thought of its having been sold to a developer who thought it was fully developable and the pressures on town boards that would have ensued. The thought of probable septic system failures and their impact on Sandy Pond, the town's principal water supply, needs no elaboration. As it turned out all parties concerned can feel comfortable that ownership of an important parcel was conveyed into vital public ownership at fair value reasonably determined.

The fourth major initiative to germinate from the 1977 land-use conference is a town effort to participate in the conversion of a large prominent parcel while creating an option for some elderly housing. As a result of the Planning Board's Neighborhood Lot Program it was learned that a 48-acre farm designated as land of conservation interest was to be sold earlier than had been assumed by the Conservation Commission. Believing the land to be owned by Mr. and Mrs. Umbrello, who are both in their eighties, the commission did not expect the land to be sold in their lifetime in order to minimize capital gains taxes. One should never make such assumptions. As it turned out the Umbrellos had placed their land in a trust for themselves and their four children, and the trustees wanted to sell the land. Since the town had indicated its interest, however, the Umbrellos were willing to keep it off the market for a reasonable period while Lincoln considered its purchase.

Made up of 12 acres of good farmland, a stream that runs

toward the town's nearby well site, some wetland, a small pond, and rolling woodlands overlooking the entire piece with long frontage along a quiet road, the entire parcel had been designated as being of conservation interest because of its need for more sensitive treatment than could be expected from a conventional subdivision. As it turned out, the Donaldsons, owners of 37 acres that abutted the Umbrellos' piece in its well site side, were also considering their piece for development because of its increased taxes under the new 100 percent assessment.

To demonstrate its interest in the Umbrello land, the commission immediately responded to the family's notification that the trust was anxious to sell by testing the property for its on-site sewage disposal potential and ordering two appraisals. The goal was to determine where the land was buildable, where this was in conflict with conservation values, and the overall value of the parcel.

After several meetings with the Umbrellos and several mutually agreed upon postponements, the commission approached the March 1979 Town Meeting with the understanding that failure to act by the town would result in the land being offered for conventional development. By this time the land had been divided into three categories for planning purposes: 12 acres of farmland that should be protected, a core piece suitable for a cluster of elderly housing units, and a few single-family lots or simply for single-family lots, and the rolling woodlands on the quiet road for single-family lots, probably in clusters. The strategy that evolved was to have the town purchase the farmland and apply for 50 percent state reimbursement, and, conditional on that, have the Rural Land Foundation commit to purchase the balance over the development period. The idea was then to have the Rural Land Foundation retrieve its initial payment by the sale of a few lots on the quiet road while a blue-ribbon housing committee prepared plans for elderly housing units to be considered at a subsequent Town Meeting. Failing to get a two-thirds vote to rezone this part of the land for such development, the Rural Land Foundation's fall-back position would be to subdivide this portion into single-family lots. The hope was that the Rural Land Foundation would realize sufficient funds from the sale of its parcels to give the town enough money to recover its net investment in the open field.

While the Umbrello piece was being planned in this way, the Donaldsons proceeded to retain, at the commission's suggestion, the services of a young landscape architect and his wife, a cartographer, to study their land's potential.

As the Umbrello piece was studied it became clear that the best possible solution for all concerned, including the siting of the elderly units being considered, was to deal with the Umbrello and Donaldson pieces as one. This led to the development of a combined site analysis map and meetings with the Donaldsons to determine their willingness to cooperate in a possible venture. Their land, as it turned out, divides itself into two distinct areas: one that can be developed with attractive single-family lot clusters using frontage along an existing subdivision road and the land near the Umbrellos' that would otherwise require a long and difficult access and would be adversely impacted by the siting of the density units being considered for the Umbrello piece. Planning the parcels together made it apparent that the resources to be protected in both parcels could be saved in a long and broad swath while the development value of the two parcels could be realized in the process of producing needed housing. By combining the two parcels the long access to the Donaldson backland that abutted the Umbrello parcel could be approached by a short connection to the site on the Umbrello land being considered for development. Developing the two parcels as one could translate this savings to the development cost of the Donaldson land into a contribution to the development of the Umbrello land.

Since the Umbrello land was fully priced, it took the innovation of having the town acquire the farmland to provide the cushion necessary to interest the Rural Land Foundation in what would otherwise be too risky a venture to undertake. In buying this piece the town would not only assure protection of the valued farmland but would stand a good chance of recovering its investment. It would, in effect, be controlling the development of 85 acres valued together at more than $600,000 and construction valued at an estimated $3 million. As we moved toward the March 1979 Town Meeting with this proposal, those of us working on it believed that the opportunity to harness this economic force to the service of multiple town needs alone justified the town's investment in the purchase of the parcel's 12 acres of farmland.

Fortunately, everything came together during the ten days prior to Town Meeting. Neighborhood hesitancy was overcome in the course of public hearings, a public walking of the land, and several neighborhood meetings. Town boards including the selectmen, the planning board, and the finance committee endorsed the Conservation Commission proposal along with the League of Women Voters.

The key, however, was an agreement in principle reached between representatives of the Umbrello family and the Rural Land Foundation on price and terms for the balance of the Umbrello land. In brief, they agreed that if the town voted to purchase 11.3 acres for $100,000, the Rural Land Foundation would purchase the balance for $300,000 as follows. The Umbrello Trust would accept a mortgage to be paid at the rate of $100,000 per year starting two years after the town's payment of $100,000, with interest to start only after the passage of these first two years. There would be, of course, release provisions so that any prior sales by the Rural Land Foundation would flow in large measure to the Umbrello Trust. In this way, the Umbrellos could expect to get their money faster although the Rural Land Foundation limited its exposure to a possible downturn in the housing market.

As it turned out, the day before the Town Meeting it was learned that the 11.3 acres to be purchased by the town were appraised at $89,000. This meant that the Rural Land Foundation would have to join the town with its own $11,000 at the closing scheduled to take place within ninety days of the town vote. Since the Rural Land Foundation had a $15,000 balance, this meant their cash would be tight. Nevertheless, at a quick meeting called before the start of Town Meeting, the trustees of the Rural Land Foundation agreed to make up the $11,000 difference.

Later that day, after a careful thirty-minute presentation and full open discussion, the Town Meeting voted unanimously to purchase the 11.3-acre open field thus essentially assuring effective control over the future of the whole Umbrello piece and a good chance for the integrated development of the abutting Donaldson 37-acre parcel. In closing my part of the presentation, I noted that we had budgeted $600,000 for the protection of the Umbrello and Donaldson land in our 1977 Open Space Plan. It now looked like a $44,500 town commitment after probable 50-percent state funding support would result in the achievement of the town's conservation goals on both parcels while providing creative options for special housing. Moreover, there was a good chance that even this amount would be returned if the Rural Land Foundation succeeded in disposing of their piece for more than $311,000 and their development costs.

We now go back to the spring of 1977. Having passed over all its articles at the March Town Meeting in favor of their consideration at a special June meeting, the Conservation Commission set out to update its year-old open space plan in light of all that had since been learned and achieved. It was most encouraging to learn that in the less than two years since preparation of the 1976 Open Space Map 100 of the 1,400 acres designated as land of conservation interest had been acquired by the town or otherwise permanently protected. Another 400 acres had been temporarily protected through conservation restrictions of limited duration or participation in the Massachusetts preferential agricultural assessment program. Only 85 acres of Lincoln farmland remained unprotected in any way and this included 12 acres of Umbrello land. Moreover, it was increasingly clear that the town's conservation goals could be achieved on several large parcels through density and cluster development. As a result it was determined that instead of requiring a $4.5 million program to achieve the town's open space and water supply goals, $2 to $3 million now seemed more than adequate.

The interim report detailed 29 major parcels for special consideration, reiterated the reasons for their importance, and suggested approaches for the protection of their vital resources. This time the acquisition costs were calculated on a worst-case basis, assuming no federal or state support, and took into account the incremental cost of managing the land to be acquired and the opportunity cost of net taxes over expenses that could be expected if the land were developed. These comprehensive costs built up to a maximum of close to $300,000 in fiscal 1987 and decreased from there, as shown in table 3.

The interim report went on to project over ten years the overall costs and cash flow requirements of conducting the town's conservation program with and without the remaining acquisitions. As shown in table 4, these costs were related to the town's 1978 tax levy so that taxpayers could consider the program in terms of its probable impact on their respective property taxes. The maximum projected impact of 10 percent, for example, would cost $150 that year to a family that would otherwise pay $1,500 in taxes. Even this large impact, it was felt, was a reasonable investment to complete the protection of Lincoln's natural systems. Moreover the impact was overstated by whatever contribution would be made by expected new housing. Over $140,000 of the $300,000 peak projected for 1987 should be forthcoming from the 58 Lincoln Ridge condominiums. Other structured growth that more than pays its way in property taxes could well lift the entire burden from Lincoln's present residents. Lincoln's approach means that future growth can be expected to make a substantial contribution to the cost of protecting the natural resources it threatens. Although it couldn't be promised in the interim report, the town has good reason to have faith in its ability to afford active participation

TABLE 3

Annual Fiscal Impact of $3 Million Acquisition Program

With initial 2-year funding leading to 20-year bonding at 5%. Figures are on a worst-case basis with no allowance for state and federal funding (all figures in $000).

	1978/79	1979/80	1980/81	1981/82	1982/83	1983/84	1984/85	1985/86	1986/87	1987/88	1999/2000	2000/01	2001/02
Projected Acquisitions[1]	$500	$1000	$500			$1000							
Short-Term Funding, 3%	15	30	15			30							
2-Year Borrowings	485	970	485			970							
Cumulative 2-Year Borrowings	485	1455	1455	$485		970	$970						
Net Long-Term Borrowing													
1978-79 Acquisitions			461	437	$413	389	365	$341	$317	$293	$221		
1979-80 Acquisitions				922	874	826	778	730	682	634	96	$48	
1980-81 Acquisitions					461	437	413	389	365	341	52	28	
1983-84 Acquisitions								922	874	826	336	288	$240
Principal Payments													
1978-79 Acquisitions			24	24	24	24	24	24	24	24	24		
1979-80 Acquisitions				48	48	48	48	48	48	48	48	48	
1980-81 Acquisitions				24	24	24	24	24	24	24	24	24	24
1983-84 Acquisitions								48	48	48	48	48	48
Total Annual Payments			24	72	96	96	96	144	144	144	144	120	72
Cumulative Bonding			461	1359	1748	1652	1556	2382	2238	2094	488	364	240
Total Debt	485	1455	1916	1844	1748	2622	2526	2382	2238	2094	488	364	240
Interest at 5%	24	73	96	92	87	131	126	119	112	105	24	18	12
Annual Fiscal Impact (3% funding + Principal + Interest)	39	103	135	164	183	227	222	263	256	249	168	138	84
Management and Maintenance (increase cost net of use receipts)		nominal—resource receipts expected to offset increased costs on overall basis											
Opportunity Costs[2]	5	15	20	20	20	20	30	30	30	30	30	30	30
Comprehensive Fiscal Impact	44	118	145	184	203	257	252	293	286	279	198	168	114

Notes: [1]Peak estimates, subject to shifts in amounts and timing.
[2]Allowance for lost tax revenue from undeveloped land and potential net contribution of $200 per preempted house per year—see text. Included for illustrative purposes. Will be estimated in detail for each acquisition as proposed.

TABLE 4

Ten-Year Conservation Program Cost Projections
With and Without Proposed Acquisition Program

| | Present Program | | | | Proposed Program | | |
	Administration, Net Maintenance & Management[1]	Debt Service	Total	As % of Tax Levy[3]	Comprehensive Costs[2]	Combined[4]	As % of Tax Levy[3]
1978/79	$45,000	$87,000	$132,000	3.7	$44,000	$176,000	4.9
1979/80	45,000	84,000	129,000	3.6	118,000	247,000	6.9
1980/81	45,000	80,000	125,000	3.5	145,000	270,000	7.5
1981/82	48,000	32,000	130,000	3.6	160,000	290,000	8.1
1982/83	48,000	31,000	80,000	2.2	203,000	283,000	7.9
1983/84	48,000	30,000	78,000	2.2	257,000	335,000	9.3
1984/85	50,000	29,000	79,000	2.2	252,000	331,000	9.2
1985/86	50,000	28,000	78,000	2.2	293,000	371,000	10.3
1986/87	50,000	27,000	77,000	2.2	286,000	363,000	10.0
1987/88	52,000	26,000	78,000	2.2	279,000	357,000	10.0

Notes: [1]Net of resource revenues.
[2]From table 3.
[3]1978 tax levy = $3.6 million.
[4]Total cost of present program plus proposed comprehensive costs.

in the conversion of its remaining privately owned undeveloped land.

I recently toured 87 acres behind Walden Pond, owned by the J. Quincy Adams family, with Quincy, two state representatives, and a representative of the Nature Conservancy. After two years of study the time has come to convey this land into public ownership to complete the protection of a broad survey of Americana. As we walked I found myself explaining how everything we did was part of a comprehensive plan that integrated the present with the past and linked Minuteman National Park to Walden Pond while providing good living space for a vital and growing community playing an important open space role in its metropolitan setting.

As I looked at Quincy I could see the unmistakable physical characteristics of his ancestors and could sense his need to keep faith with his grandfather, Charles Francis Adams, who had acquired the family property in 1894, by conveying this part of it into public use. Although he didn't mention it, I knew Quincy was thinking of CFA's dream of a ring of parks around Boston. The original plan for a park on the Lincoln-Waltham border had failed. So what! Quincy was key to a better one. As we swung from Walden over the Fairhaven cliffs, I was intensely aware of the importance of what we were about. It was a beautiful fall day. As we walked Quincy pointed to the place where Thoreau is supposed to have accidentally started a fire while cooking a pickerel. Then he shifted to self-guiding trails and the joys of cross-country skiing that might be enjoyed by regional residents.

As Quincy's dog Sassy splashed in a small pond we talked about the unauthorized use of his land and the problems with intruders who drove in, built fires, and partied all night. We talked about the need for management and control and how to achieve it without destroying the experience of being alone in the woods.

As we walked I even found myself telling of being moved by reading *The Last Angry Man* when I was in the Navy twenty-two years earlier. I recalled how this doctor in Harlem had survived with the thought that there was at least one place, Walden, that was unspoiled, and how, upon visiting it, he had become distraught to find it spoiled by a trailer court and other intrusions. But now it was all being made right. An effective restoration program is under way. The state has acquired the trailer court and is planning the relocation of the highway that runs along Walden so that it will no longer violate that special place. In Lincoln, at Walden, where so much of our country's history is rooted, we are proving that America's land use future doesn't have to be all downhill. There are ways to build healthy communities in harmony with their natural setting. It can be done. We are proving it.

I hate to bring this chapter to an end without telling about all the other projects: the citizens' preservation of the Old Town Hall; the restoration of old town-owned barns dating back to the 1790s with timber taken from Lincoln's conservation lands in the process of applying good forestry practices; and our spreading system of bicycle paths. There are so many anecdotes to tell. My involvement in the Lincoln story has so enriched my life that I feel I could write endlessly about the people and the incidents that are the real history of Lincoln's land use efforts —perhaps in another book.

CHAPTER FIVE

Outreach, Teaching, and Consulting

MY LINCOLN Conservation Commission experience opened a whole new world to me. As word spread about what we were doing, I frequently found myself called to other communities to tell the Lincoln story and relate it to their needs. When I went to give my first talk I had no idea that I was setting off on an intellectual expedition that would lead me to countless speaking, consulting, and teaching engagements all over the country, or that I would gain sufficient perspective to comment on land conversion issues in the United States. The highlights described in this chapter were selected to present what I learned in context.

"Wake up . . . shape your land use destiny . . . Don't let random forces eat up your open spaces and destroy your way of life." Those were my opening words to citizens and officials of a small Massachusetts community of 3,000 people living on 13,000 acres. That was in 1971. It was my first effort at outreach. I can remember going on to say, "I'm here tonight to raise to a level of broad consciousness a little understood problem confronting many towns such as yours. I'm going to express this problem in economic and sociological as well as ecological terms. I'm going to prove to you that this problem can be solved. I'm going to suggest that you have the right—even the obligation—to tackle this problem. I will then present some approaches that have proven results. And, finally, I'm going to offer to help in any way I can because yours is a common problem that we must all solve together if our region is to make sense to us as well as to future generations." I can cite these words verbatim because I was so nervous that I had written them down. Later they were published by Massachusetts Audubon along with the rest of my talk. I went on to describe the town as I recalled it, looked into its land use future, and recommended a course of action. The talk still rings true. It went as follows:

As I see it your town is still much as it was when I first began coming here to enjoy its scenic beauty some ten years ago. Whether or not expressed, I'm sure that most of your town citizens value its openness, quiet town roads, lovely orchards, and warm small-town ways. There is a balance in the way that man relates to nature and to his fellow man that feels good.

As I look ahead, however, I see a real threat in the form of building pressures. I see this accentuated by your new interstate highway, changes in farming economics, the national cry for another economic boom, the growth of surrounding metropolitan areas, and—perhaps of greatest importance—the filling up of other towns that have absorbed building pressure in the past.

As I see it, then, the stage is set for the rapid development of your town on a piece-by-piece basis. I see no viable action plan for saving those areas that must be saved to preserve the town's essential characteristics. I also foresee a need for rapidly expanding town services to meet future needs. School, waste disposal, and other increased costs of town government have a way of growing on a per capita basis as inflation persists. The real sadness comes when the citizens who have shaped the town find themselves unable to remain, as taxes per household spiral to accommodate the needs of new houses. I understand, for example, that a study conducted at my prompting shows that the average new house in your town falls some $750 per year short of being self-sustaining—even with existing facilities.

Should your town objectives include some or all of the following,

I see rising town costs impacting on your willingness to support these objectives.

A more favorable tax rate than those towns with which you normally compare yourselves.

Open space.

Population equilibrium—slow growth—balance between stability and enough new blood—balanced income and social groups.

Quality education.

Recognition that you are part of larger communities—your water basin region—your greater metropolitan area.

I'm here tonight to outline ways in which the objectives indicated above can be served while providing needed housing. The choice is to save those lands that should be saved—to actively determine the town's ultimate land destiny. I'm sure, for example, that your town could justify a goal of saving some 1,000 to 2,000 acres on existing knowledge alone. Let me show you how this could be done without sacrificing any of the town objectives we discussed.

Consider the economic implications of saving 1,000 acres versus their development. Let us further assume an average cost of $1,000 per acre, or a total cost of $1,000,000.

Town cost appropriated to acquire (3 percent)	$ 30,000
Federal assistance (50 percent)	500,000
State self-help (25 percent)	250,000
Town bonding (22 percent)	220,000
	$1,000,000

If the town's $220,000 portion were bonded over ten years at 5 percent, the impact on town taxes would probably be as follows:

	Year 1	Year 2	Year 11	Thereafter
Appropriation	$30,000	—	—	—
Principal	—	$22,000	$22,000	—
Interest	—	11,000	1,100	—
Total	$30,000	$33,000	$23,000	—

Given your one and one-half acre zoning, such an acquisition could relieve building pressure for 666 houses at a per house subsidization saving of $750 per year for a total of $500,000 per year.

Even if the land were to cost $2,000,000, or if only 50 percent outside assistance were available, these figures show a one-year payout as compared against the hidden cost of not saving the land.

"O.K.," some will say, "let's buy some land but let's pay for it outright."

The trouble with this conventional wisdom is that it would be impossible to levy the taxes that would be needed to do the job that needs to be done now. Moreover, since the expenditure is for land, the most permanent of assets, it is financially sound to stretch the payments over time and share the cost with future generations. Besides, the land will not be available in the future at today's prices.

Another way to contemplate such an acquisition is to think of it as though each of 1,000 families were to purchase another acre to be held in common. At $1,000 per acre, each family would acquire its acre for 250 pre-tax dollars payable over ten to eleven years. As indicated above, this would work out, with interest, to $30 year one, $33 year two, and on down to $23 year eleven. The alternatives might be for each family to subsidize two-thirds of a house at $750 per house, or $500 per year, indefinitely.

The economics involved in saving land are so one-sided that people think there must be something wrong—and there is. The fact is the theoretical savings don't totally materialize. Some of the savings can be used to do the other things the town wants to do to serve its objectives and meet its obligations. This economic leeway can be used to plan moderate-income housing, denser housing where the land will support it, and all of those other good things such as better education —and yes, lower household taxes—than there otherwise would be.

In short, it is overwhelmingly more sensible to go about building the town you really want than it is to let random forces and piecemeal thinking determine the town's destiny.

Once the town's future is given shape, you'll be amazed at the complementary activities that will develop. Should your Conservation Commission provide a meaningful backbone program, you'll find other groups and individuals fleshing it out. You'll discover the beginnings of a land trust that will collect dues and gifts of land to save pieces that might not otherwise be saved. You'll discover private groups forming tax-exempt foundations that can—through credit support only—undertake public spirited developments that fit into the town's evolving scheme. In Lincoln we find a land foundation developing a commercial area and a moderate-income development. Its profits are in the form of land given to the town. Its first project was a 109-acre piece that resulted in either new self-sustaining houses with a 54-acre gift to the town and enough residual profit to stake its other projects. I'm pleased to report that we've already put members of your Conservation Commission and other citizens in touch with this group.

Let me anticipate your questions about outside financing and the matter of possible state and federal influence.

There is a tendency to think of our towns as independent city-states whose sovereignty must be protected from state and federal governments. Let me just say that we must learn to shed this view. Nature does not recognize political boundaries. Most would agree that, from an ecological point of view, conservation programs must be implemented that transcend our political boundaries. Of less obvious significance is the fact that the involvement of the conservation agencies of the state and federal government may offer the only real protection from their road-building and other development-oriented agencies.

In summary, then, I have presented you with a way of thinking about your town. It should provide a focus for all town boards in land use matters. Its successful implementation will obviously require everybody's cooperation. In Lincoln, for example, our different committees have a practice of exchanging minutes. A recent step that should help us in our land use is the involvement of the Conservation Commission in the subdivision planning process through changes in our zoning bylaws.

The point of view presented tonight should lead to a total town planning with an ecological as well as financial point of view. In fact, your planning must transcend your town lines and reach out to your water basin and other ecological borders. You can't afford not to do it. If I had to guess where this thinking process will lead you, I can see you undertaking an environmental quality survey. By the time you're done, you'll know about your drainage, your basic water flows, present and future roads, historical areas, and appropriate land use. Maybe you'll end up preserving 4,000 acres. I would hope you'd save at least 1,000 acres.

All I can say is that it can be done. If you reach out, you'll find

encouragement at all levels of the state and federal governments—
even from your neighbors.

The talk was given serious consideration and much of what
was recommended has been implemented. Its publication,
under the title "Shape Your Land Use Destiny," by the Massachusetts Audubon Society triggered a chain reaction that
quickly took me to forty or fifty speaking engagements.[1]

At first I was pleased to go out and replay a simple version
of "Shape Your Land Use Destiny" and then deal with local
specifics in a question-and-answer period. Very soon I found
that there were too many places to go and that, to do a satisfactory job of dealing with the specifics of a town, I would have
to study its master plans, annual reports, and census data on file
at the state Department of Communities and Development.
Since this took time, I began to charge $100 for an evening
presentation. By then my talks included a slide presentation on
the evolution of land use decision making in Lincoln. I would
attempt to make a visual presentation of Lincoln's physical
setting and major development features, along the lines described in the preceding chapter. Then I would review their
community's planning as it related to open space and discuss
the losses implied in their planning and the losses that were
being suffered despite the planning. Both were usually eye-
openers. Then I would suggest a course of action for mapping
land of conservation interest with ownership lines, testing likely
futures, and developing options to resolve conflicts. I used an
overhead projector to present the economics of saving open
space in their community based on figures drawn from state and
town publications. Tax impacts of major acquisition programs
were reduced to their probable fiscal impact on average families
along the lines done in Lincoln so that individuals could stretch
their land use concerns to the borders of their community and
participate in its overall land conversion based on their priorities and ability to pay.

As these presentations grew more sophisticated, I found it

helpful to develop data on the municipal costs of saving a piece of land as compared with allowing it to be developed. Right from the start I had realized that economics was the key to saving open space. In 1971, before my first talk, I had asked the chairman of the local Conservation Commission to estimate the municipal costs of servicing the houses built in the prior three years and to compare these with the tax revenues paid by the owners of these homes. It was this study that made it possible for me to state that their average new housing was falling $750 short of paying its share of municipal costs per year. It was this figure that enabled me to demonstrate that it would be less costly for residents to save the land that needed to be saved than to have it developed.

To help other towns prepare for my talks I developed a methodology for calculating the economics of municipal growth. In November 1972 the Massachusetts Department of Natural Resources saw fit to refer to this in an article "The New Math: Conservation Equals Dollars Saved," which was sent to Massachusetts Communities. In anticipation of a flood of calls for details I wrote a brief article entitled "Comparative Economics of Conservation versus Development" for publication by the Massachusetts Audubon Society. To deal with individual community experiences, this article called for the identification of all houses built and occupied over the preceding three years, determination of their average school costs based on actual students and per pupil costs, allowance for the annual capital costs of needed new school facilities, if any, and the addition of average nonschool costs per community dwelling unit. This average total cost was then compared to the average property and excise taxes paid by those houses. The resultant net short-fall in contribution was then used to estimate the likely fiscal impact of future housing and to develop an economic comparison to the capitalized costs of purchasing the land for conservation.

This crude methodology was greatly refined in 1977 as part of a cooperative effort between me and representatives of the

Maine Coast Heritage Trust, the Maine Association of Conservation Commissions, the University of Maine, and the Maine business community. The resulting booklet took community growth and other complex factors into account; it has been widely used as a teaching aid in Maine communities.

As a sequel to "Shape Your Land Use Destiny" I wrote an article on conservation ethics because I was anxious that others who might follow the Lincoln example would do so for the right reasons. I did it simply by writing of a Lincoln summer school experience in which I had been asked to address a class of Lincoln nine- and ten-year-olds that included several black children from Boston's Roxbury section enrolled in our school's metropolitan educational program. After introducing myself to that class as the richest man in town, I told them I was rich because I owned over 800 acres of land in Lincoln. I then asked the students how much land they owned. Some said two acres; the Roxbury kids said none. After an awkward silence one child in the back of the room said he also owned 800 acres in Lincoln. "That's right," I replied, "we all own 800 acres of land in Lincoln." I went on to say that we had acquired the land because it was the best that we had and that we had saved our best so that we could share it, just as the city kids shared their community with us. To be sure, I went on, we all had an obligation to take care of this common land.

The issue of property taxes was not discovered by the proponents of California's Proposition 13. Back in 1972 I was asked to submit an article on conservation for publication in the *University of Massachusetts Technical Guidance Center Bulletin.* I took this opportunity to write some of my thoughts on the economic and cultural implications of growth and land use. Basically it was an attempt to reason why property taxes in urbanizing communities grew fifteenfold over a twenty-year period when inflation would suggest a doubling or quadrupling. My observations and hypotheses were really quite simple but they did seem to capture a causal relationship that was and is still being neglected. Basically it was observed that there is a significant difference between internal rural growth and growth from urban in-migration. In a stable rural community property taxes are a convenient way of allocating public costs to families in ways that balance out over their different family cycles. For example, young parents with children to be educated stay on to contribute to the cost of educating the children of others after their children have grown. This is often not the case with urban in-migrants who move into bedroom communities to stay only as long as the salary earner holds his job. Where the rural household pays in taxes roughly what it costs in municipal services over the course of its life cycles, suburban homes tend to be filled with families in the high municipal service cost phase of their lives. As the children of these households leave school, it is often time for the family to move on and be replaced by a family with new young children to be educated. This was particularly true in the 1950s and 1960s.

Moreover, the article noted that, as a rural community begins to suburbanize, the urban in-migrants tend to want higher quality and more expensive public services. School facilities and curricular, for example, have to be geared to the needs of the often vocal and persuasive urban in-migrants. This is seen as progress. The fact that it often entails higher property taxes that cannot be supported by the economic activities of the remaining rural elements is not perceived or considered. As a result urban in-migration often leads to the collapse of rural life which is usually rooted in agriculture. As these dynamics run their course the urban in-migrants find fewer rural families to burden with their disproportionate public costs. As rising taxes begin to catch up with their ability to support new public facilities and services, they call for spending cuts. By then, however, farmers and others of modest incomes have usually been driven from their communities or have adjusted by changing their way of life. As the rural culture dies and continuity with the past is lost, land uses compatible with long-range ecological stability are usually replaced with sprawl.

As I went from place to place to tell the Lincoln story and relate it to individual communities, it became increasingly clear that our nation could not afford to have every community follow the early Lincoln example of purchasing all the land that needed to be protected from urbanization. I could point out, as I did in 1974 to the membership of the Society for the Preservation of Cape Cod, that it would theoretically be cheaper for the residents of the Cape's fifteen towns to buy all of the remaining undeveloped land rather than to allow more housing to be built. But this was clearly impractical because it implied state and federal support programs we as a nation could not afford. Besides, the land use problems being experienced on the Cape were complex and could not be solved by a simple closing of the two bridges over the Cape Cod Canal to new residents.

By this time I was aware that a community's real growth problems were not simply a function of population growth, that they were really rooted in the way undeveloped land was being converted into residential and commercial use. We had learned in Lincoln that there were no short cuts to mapping natural systems and other public interests at a legible scale, identifying potential development conflicts, and setting out to resolve each and every one in a positive manner that fostered healthy community growth while minimizing public costs.

It was around this time that I found the following visual aid to show that there were many more options in the land use decision-making process than were usually considered, and that most of our problems stemmed from ignorance and failure to respond rather than from unavoidable givens.

Shortly after being introduced I would point to a large figure like that on page 122 and ask, "How many squares can you see?" Many would quickly respond with the number 16. After a while some would say 17. Then others would start seeing the combinations of four and say 21. Usually I would end up pointing out the remaining combinations of fours and nines which bring the number to 30. I would then make the point that we

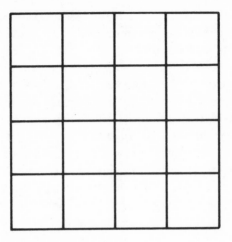

are prisoners of our perceptions—that the way we experience problems limits the choices we believe we have and as such influences the selection.

This exercise allowed me to discuss the Lincoln experience in terms of a search for new options in developing possible futures for the town's undeveloped land. We had started off with heavy emphasis on the town's purchase of complete parcels as they came to market. But, by 1978, Lincoln had learned several ways to relieve an owner of land he needed to sell, to bank it while optional futures were considered, and to foster preferred options that best met community needs.

In this way the land needs of community growth were harnessed to the task of protecting natural features that needed protection. Drawing on the Lincoln experience, for example, I would go on to show how the Farrar Pond Village and Lincoln Woods developments had resulted in the conversion of 167 acres of farmland, wetland, and rolling woods into dwelling units for 205 families of diverse incomes and backgrounds while protecting the parcels' wetlands and farmlands totaling 119 acres, at the same time making a net annual contribution of some $80,000 to the cost of municipal services.

I found that the squares were not only a land use metaphor
—I could draw on them to establish a common perception or
plane of consciousness regarding the broad importance of land.
To do this I would tell about being invited to draw on my
conservation experience to teach a Sunday School class in 1973.
After considerable thought I had decided that I would attempt
to generate a sense of self in the universe, a personal perspective
to enable the children to think of themselves in terms of the
universal and the eternal. For this purpose I brought three
items: an apple, a small flowering plant, and a trilobite.

I told the children I would make the apple talk, and proceeded to eat it. Then I asked if they could hear the apple talk.
Next I smelled the plant and said it smelled me, that I became
the plant as it became me. Finally I asked each child to touch
the trilobite and asked what possible connection there could be
between them and the small animal that had lived 600 million
years ago. I pointed out that the stuff that their fingers were
made of was every bit as old as the trilobite and went on to say
that we are our parents and grandparents, part of a long proces-
sion of life, the heavens of generations gone by, their promise
of a better tomorrow.

I believed that then and I believe it now. In my talks I would
go on to tell how it later occurred to me that the stuff of our
bodies is really comprised of elements formed in the expansion
and collapse of distant stars, that we are really children of the
universe, that, in fact, when God made the world he made us.

I remember saying this in my introduction to a paper entitled
"The Economics of Saving Massachusetts Farmland" before a
group of about 200 Northeast planners and agriculturists at the
University of Massachusetts in 1976. There were several students in the audience. When I went on to say, "Don't let that
intimidate you . . . we're all children of the universe," there was
a spontaneous roar of approval. We had achieved a common
level of understanding and trust. From then on we all knew that
it was deep to deep that we would communicate.

I then told how I had found myself thinking about my new identity the preceding October as I drove from Kennebunkport to Portland, Maine, on a conservation mission. The sun was shining brightly, warming everything. Its reflections were revealing shape and color to the natural and manmade landscape. There was an FM radio in the car playing a Beethoven concerto, making the whole scene of an early fall drive in rural Maine quite overwhelming.

All of a sudden it came to me that the sun was reaching down and touching me. I thought of Beethoven writing his music some two hundred years earlier, and in the process converting himself into a lasting energy that would span the centuries to find me driving in a remote corner of Maine. I could feel myself feeding on all that beauty, felt it nourishing me so that I could feed others with my own energy, growing in part from what I had experienced. In short I could feel the soul of Beethoven reaching me through time and space.

Before going on with my paper on Massachusetts farmland, I remarked that it was this sense of continuity and oneness, this sense that we have always been and will always be, that we have presence beyond the boundaries of our skin, that we can convert ourselves into something that we aren't—be it children, words, or music—that life goes on as long as we keep faith with the past and the future by preserving the stuff of life in its life-sustaining forms. Only then did I go on to talk about the importance of saving farmland.

And so it is with this book. The words you read are the extended me. The future of the earth's undeveloped land is my future. It is also your future and our past. We must treat it kindly. The resource prophets of today tell us that land use issues are not frivolous, that, in fact, they boil down to survival.

Although the words are always different at each of my talks the message is always the same. We are children of our habitats. When we talk land use, we talk food, water, and air; we talk about homes and jobs; we talk about hopes and dreams; we talk about the past and about ways to make the future work in the best possible way. It takes this sense of urgency and import to move people to effective involvement.

Recollections of numerous speaking engagements in Massachusetts, in each of the other New England states, in New York, Florida, Colorado, and California come to mind. In each case there was the long preparation, trying to understand the underlying problems that prompted the invitation and then searching through my experience for approaches to solutions. There was always a moment of anxiety when I first met my hosts and could sense their wonder as to whether I would live up to their expectations. This was followed by all those moments of truth when, after walking into a town or city hall, county office, church cellar or pulpit, the time arrived to address the sometimes twenty, sometimes two hundred people who had come to hear me speak about their community and how they could better shape its future. Looking back it's hard to believe the number of times this happened. In each case I met exciting and caring people; in several cases I made lasting friendships.

At first I was invited to talk in towns comparable to Lincoln. Soon thereafter I found myself relating what I had learned about land use to very different kinds of communities. The relevance of the Lincoln experience to other communities was always an issue to be confronted.

Yes, Lincoln was different. Census figures reveal that Lincoln residents have one of the highest median incomes in Massachusetts and an average education level that reaches beyond the college level. Nevertheless the town has managed to retain a goodly number of its presuburbanization families, members of which continue to exercise substantial influence in town matters. And yes, it is true that a host of caring professionals, lawyers, doctors, accountants, architects, scientists, financial types, and others have settled in Lincoln and been caught up in the pleasant chore of running their community. It is also true that the early professional in-migrants were absorbed into the rural community and set an early tone of adopting prevailing values rather than trying to bulldoze away the old-time values. As a result it seems there has always been a large pool of diverse talents and homogeneity of spirit upon which to draw in identifying and addressing community problems. The fact that Lincoln's tax rate on an equalized basis is lower than any of its abutting or neighboring communities, however, argues that it was caring and knowledge more than money that made Lincoln's creative development possible. As people in different communities come to understand this, as they come to realize that most of Lincoln's creative efforts are really quite simple, I find that anticipated barriers fall, positive communication takes place, and people volunteer to take on the needed roles.

As I moved from towns to suburbs, cities, and counties, it became apparent that what we had really developed in Lincoln was a way of thinking, a willingness to come together as a community to identify problems in community terms and to draw on community resources for their solution. Once a person in a city assessed for a total of $500 million understands that each dollar in his tax rate raises $500,000 and that a twenty-year commitment of this amount will support a $10 million land acquisition program over a twenty-year period with 50 percent state or federal assistance, he is in the conservation business. Once he understands that zoning options can be changed and that there are a number of ways in which a community can foster needed development, he is in the housing business. Once he understands the plight of local farmers and the importance of locally grown food, he is in the farming or gardening business. The same is true for water supply, waste disposal, and other land use issues. In short my message is that if people have a land use problem and haven't solved it, it's probably because they haven't tried hard enough. That's the real thrust of the Lincoln story.

The Lincoln story is also a lesson in the interplay between the private and public sectors of our society. It is a lesson in making public police powers and public programs work to meet private needs. This aspect of the Lincoln story was brought to my attention during a two-day Trust for Public Land conference held in San Francisco, where I had been invited to speak, in February 1978. After my introduction on perceptions and my telling of the Lincoln story, the sixty representatives of land trusts from Florida to Oregon broke up in small groups to share their worst problems. I found myself involved in the development of new options for ten problems, ranging in size from a few acres to over 30,000 acres. We were able to come up with new ways of seeing each problem and practical new ways of dealing with it. As the conference drew to a close someone said he had come to the conference expecting another lesson in the mechanics of dealing with land problems only to find he was going home with a sense of their dynamics.

In our small town of Lincoln we learned early of the need to involve state and federal government agencies as well as local town boards and private citizens in dealing with the conversion of our undeveloped land. In the mid-1970s, I learned that the importance of this linkage was not generally perceived.

I actually witnessed the important problem-solving chemistry that can develop when all of the parties to a land use problem are brought together in Breckenridge, Colorado, in 1973. I had been invited to address a conference of developers, county and state officials, and interested citizens. After saying something about going there a few days early to drink their mountain juices and breathe their mountain air so I could talk to them mountain to mountain, I went on to relate how we in Lincoln had been able to work with landowners and developers in allowing growth to take place while protecting what needed to be protected and dealing fairly with landowners.

Summit County was then experiencing a recreational development boom as a result of the recently completed Eisenhower Tunnel that opened up the area to quick access from Denver and Boulder. I was much impressed to watch the several participants discover that they were not natural enemies, that developers and planners, landowners, and government officials all lived in houses, drove cars, and loved the Rockies. Surely they could work together toward the wise development of the area.

Shortly thereafter I was hired as a consultant to help the Conservation Foundation develop the public-private sector focus necessary to provide management handles to the land use practices threatening Rookery Bay in Collier County, Florida. Before my involvement extensive program studies to protect Rookery Bay dealt mainly with biological, topographic, vegetative, and other physical conditions. Perceived development threats were simple extrapolations of past experiences. No one had actually gone to meet the county commissioners and planners to determine the impact of past development on the general body politic and discuss emerging political responses.

It took only three days to find out that the explosive growth that was threatening Rookery Bay was also threatening the economic and social stability of the entire county. With local help I organized a quick study of the economics of growth on Marco Island and elsewhere around Rookery Bay and found that spiraling property taxes were directly linked to the area's growth. I also learned that county officials were in the midst of developing new zoning maps that would severely restrict the growth that could take place around Rookery Bay. Shortly thereafter concerned environmentalists were working with county officials and interested citizens in shaping the area's growth. My report to the Conservation Foundation, "Growth and Land Use," was published and well received. To be sure, several of the important decisions that have since altered the negative patterns of growth in the area were settled in the courts. By this time such Rookery Bay environmental issues as the dredging and filling of mangrove swamps are being considered in a full county context, not simply in terms of a limited constituency and resource base.

The power of private-public sector cooperation in solving land use problems never ceases to astound me. The unfolding story of the preservation of the bulk of Katama Farm on Martha's Vineyard is a marvelous example of what can be achieved. In the mid-1970s this 220-acre flat, stone-free, and fertile piece of outwash plain near Katama Bay in Edgartown was destined to be converted into a speculative grid development of over 400 small lots. Before it was developed the owner went into bankruptcy.

Sensing an opportunity, the Vineyard Conservation Society mobilized a broadly representative group of public officials and private individuals to see what could be done to shape the future of Katama Farm. This group included representatives of the local business and agricultural communities, the press, and town officials. Without a set plan, and committed only to a multiple-use approach, the group decided to contact the trustee in bankruptcy and the bank holding the farm as collateral and offer to purchase an option on the land at a set price. Failing in their first offer because a better one was made by another would-be purchaser, the Vineyard Conservation Society offered to pay $40,000 for a one-year option to acquire the farm for $340,000. To avoid an auction competition, this bid was limited to two days and was quickly accepted. To pay for the option and help finance the project, the Vineyard Conservation Society solicited and quickly received gifts totaling $50,000.

Shortly thereafter I was retained as an adviser to the project. Right from the start it was my hope that the essence of Katama Farm could be protected at no net cost to the local taxpayers so that the town would not be encumbered in its ability to deal with other large parcels expected to be offered in the near future.

The plan that evolved called for Edgartown's purchase of 160 acres to be permanently dedicated to agriculture for $300,000. It was unanimously approved at the April 10, 1979, Town Meeting where it received a standing ovation. It is expected that the state will reimburse $150,000. The Vineyard Open Land Foundation, patterned on Lincoln's Rural Land Foundation, will then develop two 15-acre parcels. One parcel is to be developed in a cluster of 11 lots to be offered first to Edgartown residents. The other parcel is to be divided into six to ten parcels to be sold for recreation homes. The existing barn and five acres will

be given to the town and placed under the control of the Conservation Commission, which will make it available for farm
and compatible recreation purposes over successive five-year
periods, depending on need. The remaining twenty-three acres
will be given to Edgartown for general town purposes. Initially
this too will remain in agriculture. Its long-range future, however, will be at the discretion of the town and may include
general recreation.

It is expected that sales by the Vineyard Open Land Foundation will generate sufficient funds to repay the town's $150,000
outlay, repair the barn, and stake future rescue projects.

As Bill Caldwell, Katama resident, sage, philosopher, poet,
and member of the Katama Farm Committee wrote, "We have
gone slowly and very carefully, because we're inventing, as we
go, a methodology that might be a model for similar efforts
elsewhere in town and perhaps in other parts of the Island."
The 1979 winter newsletter of the Vineyard Conservation Society concluded its article on the Katama Farm story with,
"What a fine thing!"[2]

Before going on to my other farmland protection and water
resource experiences, I would like to make three more observations about my community involvements. The first is that it is
never too late for a community to undertake a program to
protect its natural resources. The land is always with us. It is
unfair to future generations to presume that the past has consumed the future. Sooner or later somebody will have to make
our natural systems work.

Second, whether one lives in a large city or in a less affluent
community, there are important natural resources to be protected and ways to get the job done.

Third, there are land use problems that are common to most
communities. Even so-called wealthy communities have a need
for low- and moderate-income housing.

I learned the first lesson in 1972 when I was retained to lay
out the economics of conservation in a new open space plan

being prepared for Maynard, Massachusetts. Located on the fast moving Assabet River just above Concord, Maynard had developed as a textile town in the nineteenth century. I wrote in the plan's introduction: "Like many old New England industrial villages Maynard has an aura of maturity, a feeling that time and industrial change have laid irrevocable claim to the area's natural resources; that it is too late to mount a meaningful campaign for long-range healthy land use. But this is to say that Maynard's past has consumed its future. Fortunately, the varied natural resources that early singled out Maynard as a desirable place to live and work can be saved." With the old polluting textile mills converted into office and manufacturing facilities for such fast-growing technological companies as Digital Equipment, it was possible to go on to say that "the changed economic character of Maynard no longer condemns the Assabet River to inevitable pollution. Protection of the town's network of wetlands will provide a natural fabric that will sustain a sense of openness and balance with nature. The town still has substantial tracts of dry and wet undeveloped land whose saving would protect the future water supply, provide scenic vistas and general outdoor recreation, maintain important physical links with the past, and otherwise enhance the quality of town life." The plan's economic analysis suggested that its implementation would cost the average family an average of $20 per year for twenty years. I believe it is safe to say that Maynard residents are more optimistic today about their town's long-term environmental prospects than they were in 1972.

This lesson was repeated in 1978 when I was retained by the Newton Conservators, a group of concerned citizens in the city of Newton, Massachusetts. Newton had only 1,344 acres of undeveloped land left, and there was a prevailing sense in this city of 91,000 people that they could not afford to save much of it. Although most was zoned for single-family houses, liberal rezoning practices created values that made it difficult for the city to compete for available open space. As a result growth pressures focused on undeveloped land, including golf courses, large estates, and land owned by religious orders rather than the redevelopment of declining neighborhoods.

My report pointed out that Newton's private property was assessed for close to $400 million, that as a result each dollar in the tax rate raised $400,000, and that purchase of the remaining undeveloped land at values based on existing zoning could be achieved with an economic impact of less than a dollar in the tax rate. Given Newton's low residential assessment rates, this amounted to $13 dollars per year for the average residence. In the report I argued the further principle that once a selling landowner's equity interests based on present zoning had been matched, a municipality should feel free to press for land conversion solutions that best meet public needs. Since most of Newton's undeveloped land was held by private golf clubs zoned for residential use, I recommended that this land be kept open through the careful negotiation of conservation restrictions that would enable members to realize a substantial portion of their club's potential development value in the form of federal income tax savings while keeping property taxes low. In return for accepting these restrictions, I argued that Newton should negotiate limited public rights to the golf courses.

Some of the remaining land, I argued, should be purchased at modest cost to the average Newton taxpayer. Still other open space could be protected by formulating new zoning provisions that would permit increased density in return for desirable open space. The use of some of this land to meet Newton's special housing needs while saving large portions as open space was also argued. I urged Newton officials to tour other municipalities in search of new zoning options.

My report was well received. As a result I expect that rezone petitions in conflict with Newton's open space goals are less likely to be approved. It may take time, but I believe that the future of Newton's remaining undeveloped land will not be sacrificed to random forces. This was confirmed by the subsequent purchase of the 87-acre Chestnut Hill Country Club for

$810,000 by a neighborhood group interested in keeping the land open. This could not have happened if the city aldermen had allowed a rezoning petition for high-rise apartments that would have created a value of $2.1 million.

As for the general applicability of Lincoln's comprehensive approach to identifying and protecting its natural resource base, I know of several communities that have drawn on Lincoln's experience in making their own plans. The town of Ipswich, Massachusetts, for example, with some consulting help from me, has just completed a new open space plan that categorizes undeveloped land of conservation interest in much the same way as was done in Lincoln. Over four years Ipswich citizens undertook a natural resources inventory conducted by the same extension service people who conducted the Lincoln inventory. The resultant soils, land use, and other resource maps were then used as the basis of a comprehensive open space map showing existing conservation land, institutional land, salt water marshes and inland wetlands, watershed and aquifer boundaries, property lines, and undeveloped land of conservation interest at a scale of 1 inch to 1,000 feet.

In addition to 5,300 acres of wetland, the Ipswich map identified 4,367 acres as being of conservation interest. These include 2,564 acres of farmland and 1,803 acres valued for such other resources as trail connectors and important vistas. Like the Lincoln open space plan, the Ipswich plan relies on the application of a full range of techniques for protecting land of conservation interest. Because of the town's socioeconomic make-up and present economic conditions, there is little emphasis on town acquisition. Instead the plan is oriented toward the protection of farmland, wetlands, and trail connectors. This strategy is based on the expectation of a comprehensive state-funded program to purchase development rights on farmland, interim relief through farmer participation in the state's preferential assessment program, a plea for more flexible zoning, and strict application of the state's wetland regulations. It also calls for a $2 million land acquisition program to protect special parcels. The annual impact of such a program on the average Ipswich family was estimated at $45.

The commonality of certain land use problems was driven home to me during my talk on the beautiful island of Sanibel as a guest of the Sanibel/Captive Conservation Foundation in late 1976. Ian McHarg's planning firm of Wallace, McHarg, Robert & Todd had just completed a comprehensive land use plan for the city of Sanibel, designed to promote orderly development while preserving the island's unique atmosphere and natural environment. Sanibel is an unusually beautiful resort area. Until a causeway connecting the barrier island to the Florida mainland was built in 1963, the island was a remote area with little development taking place. When the causeway was built, housing starts soared and considerable land below five-foot elevation was subdivided and sold to vacationers and speculators. By 1977 the island was under development siege, with the risk of hurricane catastrophe growing daily.

Drawing on the planning expertise of McHarg's firm, the legal expertise of Fred P. Bosselman and his associates, the environmental expertise of the Conservation Foundation's John Clark, and others, the Sanibel plan relies heavily on community police powers to eliminate building potential in certain hazardous areas and reduce it severely in others. Having read this plan before my talk, I wondered what if anything was left to say. Two points came to mind. First, although the new plan, which had been adopted as a city ordinance, severely reduced the building potential of lowlands—thereby eliminating the building potential of numerous lots owned by people all over the country—Lee County continued to tax them as building lots. I wondered how the courts would deal with this in a showdown and urged Sanibel officials to go about negotiating settlements before claims became exorbitant. Second, I observed that the new plan depended more on "thou shalt not" than on the creative solution of community problems. This became particularly apparent as I spoke of Lincoln's approach to providing low- and moderate-income housing while saving valuable re- sources at no cost to the town. All of a sudden people in the audience wanted to pursue this subject further. It soon became clear that Sanibel had a need for low-income housing for island workers who have to commute to the mainland. Moreover there were pieces of land that suggested themselves for Lincoln-like treatment.

Although the talk went well, I expected little follow-on con- tact. To my surprise, however, I received a letter in late 1978 from the new mayor of Sanibel asking me to send material on Lincoln's approach to low- and moderate-income housing. It's not unusual to hear from communities a long time after a visit. Somehow, though, I had never really expected a request from Sanibel for information on Lincoln's low- and moderate-income housing.

It was less surprising to be drawn into the world food and water crises as they emerged in the mid-1970s. As the world's growing dependence on concentrated sources of food was seen to be dangerously vulnerable to climate and political change and as the switch to concentrated metropolitan water supply systems by communities in large urban areas was seen to be similarly vulnerable, Lincoln's successful strategy for preserving its farmland and local water supply became an attractive commu- nity option. By then I had no more time to give to my growing land use hobby. Seeing chances to contribute to the develop- ment of a new state policy on saving farmland and to the development of metropolitan Boston water quality plans, I sol- icited and obtained a modest funding commitment from a char- itable foundation to support my part-time work. It was this financial support that made it possible for me to prepare and deliver a paper entitled "The Economics of Saving Massachu- setts Farmland." It is this support that made it possible for me to serve as a citizen adviser to the Boston Metropolitan Area Planning Council's Wastewater Management Planning Pro- gram and to the proposed Connecticut River Northfield Diversion Study program. This support has also made it possible for me to respond to many community inquiries where local support funds are not available.

The positive response given my paper on the Massachusetts farmland was most gratifying. Not only was it published by the Massachusetts Association of Conservation Commissions and distributed to each and every Massachusetts community, but it was reprinted in whole or in part by such organizations as the Massachusetts Land League and the Tufts Environmental Center. I could tell it touched a raw nerve when I was asked to debate its economic approach with a professor from MIT before the staff of the Massachusetts Audubon Society. This paper was also part of a package circulated to Massachusetts legislators before their overwhelming vote in favor of a $5 million pilot development-rights program to save Massachusetts farmland.

This paper attempts to demonstrate that the investment of up to $150 million to protect the last remaining 700,000 acres of Massachusetts farmland, especially 300,000 acres of cropland, would provide a handsome overall return on the public's investment if combined public and private sector costs and benefits were considered. It also argued the case for numerous options to saving farmland without public expenditure and presented an option matrix similar to the Lincoln table shown in the previous chapter. Only where there is no viable option to public expenditure, I argued, should public funds be used to protect farmland. I did note that it was tough to harness the limited growth potential of most rural areas through incentive zoning because of the economics of running roads behind open fields to concentrate houses in back woods.

Nevertheless, incentives should be provided to concentrate housing in and around rural community centers to save the unnecessary costs of servicing scattered dwellings as well as saving remote farmland. Otherwise farmland is often the first to be developed because it is already cleared and usually has easy access. Where development pressure is slight the present value of money should result in low valuations for development rights in open fields that have little chance of being sold in the near future, particularly at today's high interest rates. In other words, what is the value of 100 acres that can theoretically be developed into 100 house lots in a community where only ten dwellings are built per year and lots sell for $10,000? Clearly nowhere near a million dollars. As a matter of fact, taking development costs and probable sellout period into account, a realistic appraisal may find the land to be worth only $100,000 for development purposes. If it is worth $400 an acre for agricultural purposes, its net development value per acre would be valued at $600. This is why $150 million might do the job of saving the remaining 300,000 acres of Massachusetts cropland. My interest in making sure that all these considerations are taken into account led to my being asked to chair the appraisal subcommittee of our agricultural commissioner's farmland task force; we developed the procedures and regulations for the state's purchase of farmland development rights. This in turn led to a governor's appointment to the state's Agricultural Lands Preservation Committee that will oversee implementation of the Massachusetts development rights program.

Although I could go on telling stories about the enriching experiences that my new-found farmland interests have brought me, there are two in particular that seem to speak to the purposes of this book. About two years ago I was invited to lead a graduate seminar session at the University of Massachusetts College of Food and Agriculture. As I prepared for the class it occurred to me to lead off with a short quiz. You can imagine the response when, upon being introduced, I handed out sheets of paper with ten questions to be answered in five minutes. The first question, of course, asked about the number of squares they could see in my little window. Next I asked about the number of acres in Massachusetts, about the number of farms, and the number of acres in food production. I asked how much food was consumed in Massachusetts and how much of it was locally produced. As you might guess, the range of answers was astonishing. It was clear to me that the trend toward specialization had failed to produce a student constituency for protecting farmland in Massachusetts. And yet, as Jean Mayer was later to point out in a talk before the Northeast Association of Agricultural Secretaries, our nation's land grant colleges hold an educational monopoly on food production and dietary matters in this country. He went on to say that in creating this monopoly the Morill Act, which gave birth to our system of land grant colleges in 1862, set the stage for the evolution of a generation of Americans largely ignorant of their vital food and dietary needs. No wonder the U.S. farmer feels ignored and abused. We live in a country that sees agriculture as food production, not processing and consumption. Someone should ask Dr. Mayer what can best be done to close the gap between our food and nutritional requirements and the American public. If I had to rely on my Yale and Harvard Business School education for the basics of how to grow me, I would doubtless have poisoned myself a long time ago. Also, I would probably be out there fighting for another shopping center on still another cornfield.

One of the things that I would like to see develop from this book is an educational center that will integrate the many disciplines that relate to sound land use and the building of healthy communities. When I consider how the Harvard Business School, for example, gives students a grasp of the functional aspects of managing a business enterprise in a changing world, I dream of a similar institution for our community planners and administrators. After all, America's business is really not business, in spite of what Calvin Coolidge once said. As in any society our real business is the building of healthy settlement patterns. We pass a lot of money through our families and corporations, but if we ask where the principal capital of our society is invested, we end up listing buildings and roads, sewers and public utilities—indeed our whole man-made physical world. This is the real stopping place of our investments. This is where we as a culture make the long-lasting commitments that will either see us through or fail us in the tough years that always seem to lie ahead.

As in the case of food production and dietary needs, a case can be made that flawed perceptions are at the root of America's rapidly increasing water problems. As a basically urban-suburban society we habitually take abundant good clean water for granted. Most of us do not understand the hydrological cycle that provides this most important of our life support elements and are not even aware of the stresses that our growth and settlement patterns are generating against once abundant ground and surface supplies. Again, how can we consider ourselves educated when we are not intimately familiar with a life support element as fundamental as water?

Water certainly wasn't something that concerned me before moving to Lincoln in 1960. The significance of Lincoln's being at the top of three watersheds was something slowly drummed into me by my fellow conservation commissioners. It took a while, but I finally started to see how rain falls upon Lincoln, drains through certain areas, collects in others, and flows into other communities. As time went on I became aware of our per capita consumption patterns and the safe yields of our main supply sources located within town boundaries. I also became aware of Cambridge's reservoir system, which lies in Lincoln and three abutting communities and provides 20 million gallons of water daily to Cambridge citizens.

The full importance of Lincoln's water situation to the long-range future of the town became apparent as we learned that the alternative to self-reliance was application for connection into the already overburdened Metropolitan District Commission system. That is when Lincoln's open space planning included a serious search for potential well sites and their protection. By this time, prospects for water shortages in eastern Massachusetts were such that the MDC moved to implement plans to augment its sources by diverting the Connecticut River as it flows through western Massachusetts. In order to add what had been learned in Lincoln and the metropolitan Boston wastewater management planning process, I accepted appointment to the Citizens' Advisory Committee organized to represent the public interest in the required environmental impact study process.

Although this work has just begun, it is clear that the cumulative failure of our eastern Massachusetts communities to provide separately for their long-run water needs has generated complex and deep-rooted conflicts with communities in the western part of the state and downstream Connecticut. The scope of the study goes well beyond determination of the environmental impacts of the ten-mile tunnel required to deliver water from Northfield, Massachusetts, to the MDC's Quabbin Reservoir near Worcester. In addition to requiring careful determination of the proposed diversion's environmental impacts on the donor and recipient systems, careful accounting of the recipient area's present uses and field justification of demand increases will be required.

Back in 1974, when I was but dimly aware of the possible diversion project, I spoke before the annual meeting of the Connecticut River Watershed Council. I opened with the remark: "I am pleased to be able to come from Lincoln with the promise that at least one town in eastern Massachusetts will so manage its affairs that it won't come knocking on your door for water. I wish I could say the same for the others." Through my participation in the Northfield study I can at least help make sure that any diversion will be adequately justified and well done.

Since the process of developing several options for each of Lincoln's owners of land of conservation interest took into account the interests of landowners, it was not long after publication of Lincoln's open space plan in 1977 that landowners in other communities called to retain my services. By this time I had come to know and work with Warrent Flint, Jr. (a descendant of a long line of Lincoln Flints) and his wife Margaret. He is a professional landscape architect and she is a professional cartographer. One of Warren Flint, Jr.'s first jobs after his graduation from the Rhode Island School of Design (RISD) was to help our Conservation Commission produce its 1977 plan. In this and other work I had come to realize that the development of an option matrix for a parcel of land could not be undertaken without careful articulation and mapping of its natural features and development possibilities. Only then could the land's carrying capabilities be related to community needs and other marketing possibilities. And only then could appraisal work and the application of income and estate tax considerations take place. Before long I was convinced that a substantial portion of our society's land use problems stems from a long history of narrowly focused planning and decision making. The options made possible by effective estate planning alone boggle the mind.

The kinds of problems our approach allows owners to deal with so far include rational separation of land to be developed and land to be protected; best means of achieving protection with minimum loss of maximum development potential values; best means of development to achieve development value potential; the conversion of undivided family interests into individual ownerships; determination of whether conservation restrictions should be established on parcels by one generation or another; the minimization of estate taxes through the establishment of irrevocable trusts and subsequent gifting of land interests; and the whole matter of relating land disposition to the task of maximizing the estate tax flow-through of liquid assets as well as land desired to be retained by family interests.

What we have found, in short, is that by careful articulation of land features at a legible scale of 1 inch to 200 feet, by superimposing development and land protection options over maps showing soils and other development limitations, and by translating these options into before and after income and estate tax dollars, it is possible to empower owners to make well-reasoned land disposition decisions. This eliminates much of the pressure for forced sales that have so often been the root cause of development that is wanted by neither owners nor local communities.

At several points along the way I have availed myself of speaking engagements to integrate and synthesize all that I have learned about the proper use of land. My first real effort was an address entitled "Growth, Land Use, and Common Sense," presented to the eastern regional meeting of The Nature Conservancy in March 1975. Much of what is in this book was foreshadowed in that talk. I paraphrased a saying attributed to Chief Justice Holmes as follows: "Every now and then, a new idea comes along to stretch your mind and it never returns to its earlier shape." At the time I had just finished studying "The Costs of Sprawl," a major publication by the Council of Environmental Quality (CEQ) which deals with the hard choices this nation faces in its accommodation of growth. Based on data in the CEQ publication, I had calculated that the accommodation of 46 million more Americans through sprawl would consume 2 million more acres and cost $200 billion more than the 4 million acres and $475 billion in total capital costs that would be required to accommodate them in a planned fashion. I pointed out that these were just the initial savings and did not include enormous savings in operating and carrying costs as well as energy conservation to be derived through compact settlement patterns.

After covering my experiences in Lincoln and other communities, I went on to call attention to Tom Paine's Revolutionary War pamphlet "Common Sense." It was written some six months after the battles of Lexington and Concord when the colonials were disorganized, the war was going badly, and there was considerable debate over reconciliation with Britain. I told how, in a few short pages, Paine had exploded the myth of King

George's divine claim to America's allegiance and of the ultimate need to separate from Britain. In my reading of our history it was Paine's "Common Sense" and his "Crisis Papers"
that united the colonials and galvanized colonial sentiment into
a winning effort.

I also went on to point out that we are going through environmental revolution not unlike that which gave birth to our nation. I said the time for destroying wetlands, prime forest, and
agricultural lands is long past. It does not make sense to destroy
the natural resource base that will be needed to support our
growing population in an inevitable age of scarcity. Fortunately, I concluded, all that is required of us is the application
of a little common sense in a determined way to achieve optimum land use in our communities.

My next major synthesis was in November 1976, when I was
asked to deliver a Carolyn B. Haffenrafer Lecture at the Rhode
Island School of Design. For this lecture I had prepared a slide
presentation to demonstrate the results of Lincoln's land use
process, including the option matrix and cash flow analyses that
demonstrated the economic feasibility of fostering community
development that meets human needs in harmony with their
natural environment. This address led to my being invited to
teach a six-session evening course at RISD on the economics
of land use in the fall of 1977 and again in 1978. These experiences in turn convinced me of the need for this book and
provided its general pattern. They also provided me with a
sense of the need to broaden the learning experience of our
planners so that they may develop functional understanding of
the many disciplines that can and should be brought to bear in
the land conversion process. How can we expect our planners
to develop a full range of creative options for their clients if they
are not familiar with all the elements that should be considered
in the land conversion equation? Again, I believe there is a need
for a graduate center that does for planning what the Harvard
Business School does for corporate planning—provide students

with a sense of the whole in making complex decisions. We must train our planners and public administrators in all the aspects of fostering sound communities. The next chapter is offered as a start in that direction.

CHAPTER SIX

The Creative Process

IT'S ONE THING to describe America's land and water resources and the growth pressures that threaten them; it's quite
another to describe the evolution of a creative response, evolved
in one community, that shows signs of being replicable elsewhere. And it's still another to attempt to reduce this process
to the beginnings of a discipline that can be studied and applied
in a wide range of different circumstances.

To protect threatened natural resources at the local level
while releasing land needed for development, I have reduced
what I have learned to the following steps.

1. For your municipality, identify and map all undeveloped
land on a base map that shows basic topographic and man-
made features. A scale of 1 inch to 1,000 feet is the coarsest scale
recommended. Preliminary work should be done at 1 inch to
200 feet. Needed base maps may be prepared from National
Geodetic Survey maps which are usually scaled at 1 inch to
2,000 feet.

2. Adjust your assessor maps to your working scale and add
property lines to your base map or develop a clear laminate
overlay showing present property lines and zoning.

3. Identify and map as land of conservation interest the land
that makes up your municipality's natural systems or has the
potential to enhance these systems. All wetlands and aquifers,

farmland, prime forest land, major wildlife areas, special vistas, and trail connectors should be included. Together they should form a cohesive natural framework on which to build your community.

4. The first three steps should enable you to determine the development potential that may be in conflict with your natural systems and appraise dollar values for the owners involved. This step should include an estimate of the net dollar value of each parcel of public conservation interest to its owner after state and federal capital gain taxes. This information may be provided along with guidance in the estate tax implications of each owner's land disposition options when discussing specific parcels. By this time a separate card or file should exist for each parcel of conservation interest.

5. The development pressures on each owner of land of conservation interest can now be studied and likely futures considered in light of each parcel's, and its owner's, particular circumstances. This step should include a possible timing of the events that would lead to conversion in order to provide a sense of available response time.

6. The preceding steps should permit a comprehensive summation of your community's land of conservation interest in terms of component composition such as cropland, aquifers, and so forth, the number of individual parcels and total acreage involved, its probable dollar value, and the probable rate of loss of important features if nothing is done to change the way land is converted in your community.

7. The next step is to determine the special development needs of your community so that these may be satisfied in the process of protecting important natural features. This may be done through a questionnaire process.

8. Set forth the economics of protecting undeveloped land in your community. Determine how even one dollar in your municipal tax rate would allow your community to begin shaping its land use destiny. Deal with the question of essential municipal priorities, and compare them to present spending practices.

Consider what portion of your municipality's overall spending would be a reasonable amount to budget for the protection of its natural systems.

9. Prepare an option matrix for enabling owners of undeveloped land to realize their full and fair dollar value by packaging the land for appropriate residential, commercial, and public interests. As in the Lincoln experience, this may well call for the development of new zoning options and the creation of new organizations like our Lincoln Land Conservation Trust and Rural Land Foundation. Be sure to factor in all available state and federal support programs.

10. Arrange a public conference to share what has been learned about the probable and possible futures of undeveloped land in your community. It may be that you will first want to publish your findings as a draft open space plan. Out of this should come a public consensus of what is needed for your community to shape its land use destiny, not only in the way of protecting wetlands, farmland, and other natural features but in providing land for needed development. The resultant goals should also lead to an appropriate budget priority for the whole task of planning and overseeing your community's land conversion process.

11. As individual parcels come up for conversion, devote the time and resources necessary to develop a clear understanding of their optional futures and press for those that make the most overall sense.

12. Do not wait until you have developed a detailed comprehensive plan for dealing with undeveloped land before involving yourself in the land conversion process. Work with what you've got at the time. Many of the growth-guiding considerations presented in this book do not require broad community participation or involvement. Most of them simply require awareness and common sense.

I have tried to show that the United States is confronted with the task of accommodating an increase in population of 40 to

80 million over the next twenty to thirty years, yet this must be done without serious further loss or degradation of its remaining natural resource base and without bankrupting itself in the process of saving the land that needs to be saved. As we begin to understand the limits of our energy, land, and water resources it is increasingly clear that this cannot be achieved without substantial change in our land conversion practices. We simply cannot allow present or coming generations to sprawl indiscriminately over our prime farm and forest land or pollute our water resources. And we can't afford to pay full ransom for sheltering these resources from unwanted development.

In the absence of an effective national land use policy we seem to be confronted with a choice between compensating owners of our vital resource land by restricting its conversion into competitive development uses or simply denying owners the right to realize maximum values through noncompensatory restrictions.

Since paying to protect one piece of resource land can merely deflect threatening development to an equally vital piece, a simple compensatory protection program must provide for the ransom of all resource land to be protected, even though overall development needs could not possibly endanger the total resource land to be protected. That's the unfortunate cost of protecting a total resource base when we can afford no further losses. And that's about where the United States is today in terms of its prime farm, forest, and aquifer land.

It has been estimated that it might cost $1 trillion to totally restrict conversion of America's 400 million acres of cropland. A country already struggling with over $800 billion in national debt cannot afford to commit itself totally to such a burden, let alone the cost of protecting other vital resource land on a compensatory basis.

Although more politically appealing at first blush, the alternative of preventing loss of resource value through noncompensatory zoning is equally fraught with danger. Can you really deny a farmland owner the right to sell his land for house lots without compensation for his economic loss? Although the question is yet to be resolved in our highest courts, states like Oregon are betting their land use future on this approach. To me this is an economic time bomb that could make the Indian claims look insignificant.

As matters stand, the United States are rapidly opting for one or the other or a combination of these two protection approaches. The only alternative appears to be continued loss of needed resource land, which will force the price of the resource products we buy to rise to a level where the land that produces them may also continue to rise in competition with possible development. If nothing is done the free market will take care of the problem by driving food prices to a level that makes it more profitable to keep farmland in agriculture than to convert it into house lots. But we may not be able to afford that either.

Fortunately, Lincoln's and other experiences prove that there are plenty of other options that should enable us to satisfy our growing population's residential and commercial land needs without having to sell ourselves into slavery or deny fair value to our landowners. But that's Lincoln, you say. If you are still doubtful, consider an ancient proverb found in one of my father's old calculus books: "What one fool can learn, so can another." Before we commit ourselves totally to programs that could end up costing more than we as a nation can afford, let's develop creative approaches to our land conversion problems in ways that save needed resources while facing head-on the job of building desirable settlements. To be sure, compensatory techniques and appropriate regulation will have roles to play in such a strategy.

To assure the future of our nation's vital land and water resources, we must embark on a program of identifying and mapping our resources as national necessities, assessing the likely futures of individual parcels, testing those against our needed resource base, and developing viable options for resolving conflicts. As in Lincoln's experience, it is to be hoped that the economic vitality of the land use needs of present and future generations can be harnessed to the task of their protection. To the extent that the Farrar Pond Village, Lincoln Woods, and Lincoln Ridge experiences can be replicated, America's agricultural and water resources can be protected at minimum out-of-pocket public cost while needed settlement options are created.

Much of the data required to establish the needed inventory of America's land of conservation interest exists or is readily available. Satellite photographs may be used to identify and map resource land and to monitor change. Local assessors can provide ownership data. Local governments can provide zoning and other settlement constraints. Census data and related projections will show growth pressures area by area. The Massachusetts growth policy experience of involving all communities should be repeated in all our states. The possible futures thus revealed should provide the data base necessary to assure the United States a desirable land use destiny.

Much of the needed data is already available from the EPA's wastewater management planning program. The USDA is preparing a farmland inventory. Extension of this kind of comprehensive planning to include other vital resources should not unduly stretch our planning resources. Building on existing public participation networks, such a planning effort can provide the American people what they need and want: a chance to consider all of our resources and participate in their needed protection. I hope this book will help bring about such a planning effort.

Although the growth-guiding approach offered in this book will work to protect natural resource land in the absence of national and state growth policies, such policies would be most helpful in supporting and reinforcing appropriate local land conversion. It is now widely recognized that much of our loss of needed land and water resources can be traced to uncoordinated federal and state spending programs. When I think of the sources of sprawl, for example, I think of GI mortgages, state and federal airport and road building, waste treatment facilities, and federally sponsored urban rehabilitation. It's not that I don't acknowledge the needs that brought forth these programs. It's simply that these same needs could have been better met through prior comprehensive planning and consideration. We cannot afford to repeat the errors of the past in preparing for the next 80 million Americans.

As citizens, landowners, developers, and local communities come to recognize the importance of creative land conversion, I hope that our state and federal governments will undertake comprehensive planning efforts that result in solid growth policies based on real resource inventories and population data. By starting now, and working from the ground up, citizen participation at the local level should help produce results that are adequate, practical, and politically acceptable. Completion of a first round of individual state planning should generate planning outlooks that can be shared and tested for conflicts by neighboring states. Resulting state and regional outlooks can then be assembled into a national land use outlook to be balanced for internal consistency. Out of such a process should come appropriate urban and rural development policies and programs to support the development of desired settlement patterns.

I am well aware that the political climate does not favor a comprehensive land use planning effort along the lines proposed in 1973. I believe this is so largely because there is no general awareness of the threat to our way of life being posed by our present land conversion practices, changing global conditions, and the coming wave of growth. Moreover, most of us are not aware that there are ways of correcting the situation besides massive government regulatory or spending programs. It has been my experience that once people see what can be achieved through a little hard work and determination, once they understand the way social, environmental, and economic considerations can be linked into an effective decision-making process that both serves and harnesses growth, once they see the possibility of their own participation in a process of creative development which replaces the random development that has been destroying their communities, they have the hope and confidence needed to insist on better local development practices. It is my sense that a coordinated national growth policy that effectively deals with the future of undeveloped land must be rooted in a broad national sense of what can be done to achieve a better man-made nation that sits gently on the land.

Perhaps it is just as well that we do not yet have a national land use program. Although I'm quite sure that we are capable of mapping our resource base with sufficient accuracy to permit effective decision making, we are not ready to commit ourselves to prevalent conflict resolution options, many of which we may not be able to afford. It may also be that we are not yet ready to define and assign appropriate federal, state, and local community roles, particularly implementation roles. I'm afraid, for example, that the urgency of our growth conflicts could be used to justify a heavy-handed centralized program whose flaws we wouldn't discover until it was too late. Although it may come to pass that this is the only choice, I would much prefer to see a program that draws on broad citizen participation for its goal setting and local ingenuity for its implementation.

Since it will probably take more time than we can afford to achieve consensus on a national land use program and have it working effectively, since U.S. resources are already fairly well inventoried and growth conflicts identified, and since there are creative options to resolve many of these conflicts at the local level, I would like to move that we get on with the business of building a better country. I contend that such a start will generate the creative input to develop a workable coordinated national land use policy. Only after we know what can be done through creative means and have fully explored what can be achieved without public compensation will we have the basis to set realistic goals and to provide adequate though limited resources for their accomplishment.

In the meantime this rudimentary process for effective participation in our nation's land conversion should enable local municipalities, individual landowners, and concerned citizens to begin systematically guiding growth away from needed resources and shaping development to meet identified needs. The tools and techniques exist. All that is needed is the organization of readily available data, the development and clear articulation of otherwise unseen options, and the marshaling of resources to achieve specific goals on individual parcels up for conversion.

The importance of effective local planning and implementation cannot be overstated. Our federal government limits itself to policy setting and delivery of technical assistance in the major land use issues confronting our country. If our prime farm and forest land and water resources are to be protected it will have to be our states and local communities that carry out the protective programs. In the absence of massive funding programs and total reliance on regulatory ordinances that may prove to be unconstitutional, it may well be that the twelve steps that make up my recommended creative process comprise our best approach to accommodating U.S. growth and change while protecting our vital natural systems.

Now that mankind has reached the point where its actions are capable of destroying our natural habitat, future generations will judge us most sternly on our treatment of the land. We must start now to save the resource base that will be needed in the future.

Notes

Bibliography

Index

Notes

Chapter 1

1. Tom McCall, "The 'Interconnectedness' of Everything. An Issue Report, Conservation and New Economic Realities: Conservation and New Economic Realities, Some Views of the Future" (Washington, D.C.: The Conservation Foundation, 1977) p. 31.

Chapter 2

1. Mankind at the Turning Point, page 168.

2. U.S. Department of Agriculture, "Our Land and Water Resources: Current and Prospective Supplies and Uses" (Washington, D.C., 1974), p. vi.

3. Wendell W. Fletcher, "Agricultural Land Retention: An Analysis of the Issue, a Survey of Recent State and Local Farmland Retention Programs, and a Discussion of Proposed Federal Legislation" (Washington, D.C.: Congressional Research Service, Library of Congress, 1978), p. 4.

4. Charles E. Little, "The Case for Retaining Agricultural Land." Paper prepared for an informal workshop at the Library of Congress on February 8, 1977, p. 18.

5. Intasa, Inc., in association with Hydrocomp, Metcalf & Eddy, and Tetra Tech, and in consultation with Joe E. Moore, Jr., "Water Supply—Wastewater Treatment Coordination Study" (Washington, D.C.: U.S. Environmental Protection Agency, 1978).

6. Ibid.

7. Daniel Patrick Moynihan, Write a New Script for the Future. *Boston Sunday Globe,* August 28, 1978, p. A1.

8. Robert A. Lemire, "The Economics of Saving Massachusetts Farmland." The Massachusetts Association of Conservation Commissions, February 4, 1976.

9. William P. MacConnell and Marcia Cobb, "Massachusetts Map Down. Remote Sensing 20 Years of Change in Massachusetts Counties" (Amherst: Massachusetts Agricultural Experiment Station, College of Food and Natural Resources, University of Massachusetts, 1974).

Chapter 3

1. Thomas C. Marcin, "Outlook for Housing for Type of Unit and Region: 1978 to 2020" (Washington, D.C.: Forest Products Laboratory, Forest Service, U.S. Department of Agriculture, 1978).

2. Tom McCall, "The 'Interconnectedness' of Everything. An Issue Report, Conservation and New Economic Realities, Some Views of the Future" (Washington, D.C.: The Conservation Foundation, 1977), p. 31.

3. Henry R. Richmond, "Report to Advisory Board, Progress to Date, 1000 Friends of Oregon, January 1975–December 1977," p. 7.

Chapter 4

1. Kenneth W. Bergen, "The Rural Land Foundation of Lincoln, Mass.: Partial Development Bootstraps Open Space Preservation," Case Studies in Land Conservation (Boston: New England Natural Resources Center, 1974).

2. Ibid.

Chapter 5

1. Robert A. Lemire, "Shape Your Land Use Destiny," *Conservation Leader,* Massachusetts Audubon Society, August–September, 1971.

2. Lucy Reynolds, "The Katama Farm Story, in *Vineyard Winter Newsletter,* Vineyard Conservation Society 1979.

Bibliography

Berry, Wendell. *The Unsettling of America: Culture and Agriculture.* San Francisco: Sierra Club, 1977.

Bosselman, Fred, David Callies, and John Banta. *The Taking Issue: An Analysis of the Constitutional Limits of Land Use Control.* Washington, D.C.: Council on Environmental Quality, 1973.

Brooks, Paul. *The View from Lincoln Hill.* Boston: Houghton Mifflin, 1976.

Brown, Lester R. "Worldwatch Paper 24: The Worldwide Loss of Cropland." Washington, D.C.: Worldwatch Institute, 1978.

Bryson, Neil, and Thomas J. Murray. *Climates of Hunger.* Madison: University of Wisconsin Press, 1978.

Cahn, Robert. *Footprints on the Planet: A Search for an Environmental Ethic.* New York: Universe Books, 1978.

Dawson, Alexandra D., and Norton H. Nickerson. *Environmental Handbook for Massachusetts Conservation Commissions.* 4th ed. Boston: Massachusetts Association of Conservation Commissions, 1978.

Dideriksen, Raymond I., Allen R. Hiddebaugh, and Keith O. Schmude. "Potential Cropland Study." Statistical Bulletin No. 578, Soil Conservation Service. Washington, D.C.: U.S. Department of Agriculture.

Doucette, Robert, Sterling Dow III, Janet Milne, Patricia Solitaire,

Robert Lemire, and George Scully. *The Comparative Economics of Residential Development and Open Space Conservation.* Portland-Gorham: Allagash Environmental Institute for Research and Advanced Study, University of Maine, 1977.

Fletcher, Wendell W. "Agricultural Land Retention: An Analysis of the Issue, a Survey of Recent State and Local Farmland Retention Programs, and a Discussion of Proposed Federal Legislation." Washington, D.C.: Congressional Research Service, Library of Congress, 1978.

Healy, Robert G., John S. Banta, John R. Clark, William J. Duddleson. *Protecting the Golden Shore: Lessons from the California Coastal Commissions.* Washington, D.C.: The Conservation Foundation, 1978.

Intasa, Inc., in association with Hydrocomp, Metcalf & Eddy, and Tetra Tech, and in consultation with Joe E. Moore, Jr. "Water Supply—Wastewater Treatment Coordination Study." Washington, D.C.: U.S. Environmental Protection Agency, 1978.

Lemire, Robert A. "Growth and Land Use, Rookery Bay Land Use Studies." Study No. 10. Washington, D.C.: The Conservation Foundation, 1975.

Leopold, Aldo. *A Sand County Almanac with Essays on Conservation from Round River.* San Francisco: Sierra Club/Ballantine, 1974.

Massachusetts Office of State Planning. "City and Town Centers, A Program for Growth: The Massachusetts Growth Policy Report," Boston: Commonwealth of Massachusetts, 1977.

McHarg, Ian L. *Design with Nature.* New York: Natural History Press, 1969.

Meadows, Donella H., Dennis L. Meadows, Jørgen Randers, and William W. Bebraus III. *The Limits to Growth.* 2nd ed. New York: Universe, 1974.

Meserovic, Mihajlo, and Eduard Pestel. *Mankind at the Turning Point: The Second Report to the Club of Rome.* New York: Signet, 1974.

Nearing, Helen and Scott. *Living the Good Life: How to Live Sanely and Simply in a Troubled World.* New York: Schocken Books, 1970.

Peskin, Sarah. *Guiding Growth and Change: A Handbook for the*

Massachusetts Citizen. Lincoln, Mass.: Massachusetts Audubon Society and Norumbega Association. 1976.

Pinto, Robert J. *How to Save Taxes Through Estate Planning.* Princeton, N.J.: Dow Jones Books, 1976.

Real Estate Research Corporation. *The Costs of Sprawl.* Washington, D.C.: Council on Environmental Quality, 1974.

Regional Data Sources:

    Greater Boston, Massachusetts
        "Areawide Waste Treatment Plan for the Metropolitan Boston Area, Metropolitan Area Planning Council." Massachusetts Water Supply Policy Study, January 1977. Massachusetts Executive Office of Environmental Affairs.

    Cape Cod, Massachusetts
        "Draft Environmental Impact Statement and Proposed 208 Water Quality Plan, March 1978." Cape Cod Planning and Economic Development Commission.

    Greater Denver, Colorado
        "Clean Water Plan, July 1977, with October 1977 and March and April 1978," notations on growth guidance, regional housing plans, and area growth.

    Greater Des Moines, Iowa
        "Condensed Report on the Des Moines 208 Areawide Water Treatment Plan," March 1977. Central Iowa Regional Association of Local Governments.

    Greater Philadelphia, Pennsylvania
        "COWAMP/208 Water Quality Management Plan," April 1978. Delaware Valley Regional Planning Commission.

    Greater Portland, Maine
        "The Greater Portland Council of Governments Areawide Water Quality Management Plan," November 1977. Greater Portland Council of Governments.

    Greater Portland, Oregon
        "Planning Adoption Process of the Land Use Framework Element of the CRAG Regional Plan," May 1977. Columbia Region Association of Governments.

    Greater San Francisco, California
        "Draft Environmental Management Plan for the San Francisco

Bay Region," December 1977. Also, "Working Paper, Revised Series 3, Projections, Population, Housing, Jobs, and Land Uses, San Francisco Bay Region." 1978. The Association of Bay Area Governments.

Southwest Florida
"The Southwest Florida 208 Water Quality Management Program, A Citizen's Interim Executive Summary," April 1978. Also, "Land Use Policy Plan," April 1978. Southwest Florida Regional Planning Council.

Reilly, William K. (ed.). *The Use of Land: A Citizens' Policy Guide to Urban Growth.* New York: Harper & Row, 1973.

Schumaker, E. F. *Small Is Beautiful: Economics as If People Mattered.* New York: Harper & Row, 1973.

Sternlieb, George. *Housing Development and Municipal Costs.* New Brunswick, N.J.: Center for Urban Policy Research, Rutgers University, 1974.

U.S. Department of Agriculture. "Our Land and Water Resources: Current and Prospective Supplies and Uses." Washington, D.C., 1974.

U.S. Government Printing Office. "Hearings before the Subcommittee on Family Farms, Rural Development, and Special Studies of the Committee on Agriculture, House of Representatives, Ninety-fifth Congress, First Session on H.R. 5882." Washington, D.C., 1977.

Zuelke, Larson & Freitus. Robert Lemire, Economic Consultant. Maynard Open Space Plan. Maynard, Massachusetts, 1972.

Index

Adams, Charles Francis, 78, 110
Adams, J. Quincy, 78–79, 100, 110
Agritechnology, 27
American Land Forum, 17, 18, 27
Appropriative Doctrine, 21
Association of Bay Area Governments (ABAG, San Francisco), 48

Barnes, Art, 36
Berg, Norman A., 17
Bergen, Kenneth, 62
Berry, Wendell, *The Unsettling of America,* 18
Biniek, Joseph P., 18
Bosselman, Fred P., 134
Boston, Massachusetts, growth and land use conflicts of, 33–37
Boston Metropolitan Area Planning Council, Wastewater Management Planning Program of, 135
Braun-Eliot Report, 57, 58, 59
Brown, Lester R., 17
Bryson, Neil, 18
Bureau of Outdoor Recreation's Land and Water Conservation Fund, 66
Butz, Earl, 14
By-70 plan, 60, 65, 68
By-80 conference, 69, 70

Caldwell, Bill, 130
Cambridge reservoir system, 36–37, 139
Cape Cod, Massachusetts, 121; growth and land use conflicts in, 40–41; rapid development of, 31, 40
Chempeny, Leona, 77
Citizens' Advisory Committee, 140

Clark, John, 134

Clean Water Act, 95

Cluster development, 98–99

Coastal Conservancy (California), 49

Codman, Dorothy, 64–65, 68; purchase of property of, by Rural Land Foundation, 70–76 passim

Codman Community Farms (Lincoln, Massachusetts), 75

Codman Trust, 75

Columbia Region Association of Governments (CRAG), 51–52

"Comparative Economics of Conservation versus Development" (Robert A. Lemire), 118

Connecticut River, 35, 36, 139–40

Connecticut River Northfield Diversion Study program, proposed, 135–36

Connecticut River Watershed Council, 140

Conservation Commission (Lincoln, Massachusetts), 57, 58, 60, 61; acres of land acquired by, 64; and cluster development, 99; and Codman Community Farms, 75; and development of Lincoln's second condominium, 94–96; initiatives of, in land development and conservation, 91–92; and Lincoln Woods, 74; and Mt. Misery acquisition, 65; negotiations of, with trustees of Sandy Pond Trust, 100–102; open space plan of, 79, 82–89, 106–7; survey by, at 200-foot scale of undeveloped land, 78–79; topographic maps of, 76–77, 78; and Umbrello property, 102–5

Conservation Foundation, 27, 44, 49, 128, 134; The Use of Land, 50

Coolidge, Calvin, 138

Council of Environmental Quality (CEQ), "The Costs of Sprawl," 142

Creative development, Lincoln's, 88, 93–94, 126

Cropland availability, USDA soil conservation study of, 15–16

Dane, Lydia, 77

DeCordova, Julian, 63

Delaware Valley Region, including Philadelphia, growth and land use conflicts in, 41–43

Denver, Colorado, growth and land use conflicts in, 45–47

Denver, John, "Rocky Mountain High," 46–47

Department of Public Works (DPW, Massachusetts), 36, 67

Des Moines, Iowa, growth and land use conflicts in, 52–54

Development-rights programs, 7–8, 51

Donaldson property, 103, 104, 106

"Economics of Saving Massachusetts Farmland, The" (Robert A. Lemire), 123, 124, 135–37

Emerson, Ralph Waldo, 100

Environmental Fund, 25

Environmental Protection Agency (EPA), 6, 17, 150; on groundwater depletion, 20; water supply and wastewater treatment coordination study of, 21, 33

Evans, Frank E., 46

Farmland: economics of saving Massachusetts' remaining, 26–27, 123, 124, 135–37; federal efforts to identify and catalog, 6–7; limited availability of potential, 5, 6; protection of, by outright purchase and zoning options, 10; special emphasis on protection of, 27–28

Farrar Pond Association, 94

Farrar Pond Village (Lincoln, Massachusetts), 75, 91–92, 98, 122, 150; development of, 72–73; failure of, to integrate into neighborhood life, 96; opposition of, to development of second condominium, 94, 97; town acceptance of, 99

Federal Wildlife Preserve (Wayland, Massachusetts), 100

First National Bank of Boston, 23

Flint, Margaret, 141

Flint, Warren, Jr., 59–60, 140–41

Florida, Southwest, growth and land use conflicts in, 43–45

Frankl, Lee, 27

George, King, of England, 142–43

Groundwater depletion, 20

"Growth, Land Use, and Common Sense" (Robert A. Lemire), 142

"Growth and Land Use" (Robert A. Lemire), 128

Growth and land use conflicts, 29–33, 54; in Boston, Massachusetts, 33–37; in Cape Cod, Massachusetts, 40–41; in Delaware Valley Region (in-

Growth and land use (cont.)
cluding Philadelphia), 41–43;
in Denver, Colorado, 45–47;
in Des Moines, Iowa, 52–54;
in Portland, Maine, 37–40; in
Portland, Oregon, 49–52; in
San Francisco, California,
47–49; in Southwest Florida,
43–45

Haffenrafer, Carolyn B., Lec-
ture, 143
Hansen, Clifford, 51
Harvard Business School, 138,
143–44
Hathaway, Mary, 63
Holmes, Oliver Wendell, Jr.,
142
Housing requirements, projec-
tion of future, 29–30
Howell, James, 23
Hubbert, M. King, 3

Ipswich, Massachusetts, open
space plan in, 133–34
Isgur, Benjamin, 69

Keane, John C., 69

Land: agricultural and nonagricultural, 14; area, earth's
total, 13; ownership, kinds of,

24; protection of versus development of, 12–13. See also
Land use
Land of Conservation Interest,
78, 79, 81–82
Land use, 1–2; patterns, 5–6, 7;
population growth and, 2–4,
24; state and local government responsibility for, 6–7.
See also Growth and land use
conflicts
League of Women Voters, 105
Lincoln, Massachusetts, 31, 55–
57, 106; average income and
education level of residents
of, 125; and By-80 conference,
69–70; cluster development
in, 98–99; and Codman property, 64–65; creative development practiced in, 88, 93–94,
126; and density zoning
provisions, 71, 75; and Farrar
Pond Village, 72–73, 75, 91–
92, 94; issues and events leading to development of second
condominium in, 93–98; and
Lincoln Mall, 76; and Lincoln Woods, 73, 74–75; and
Mt. Misery acquisition, 65–
68; and negotiations with
trustees of Sandy Pond Trust,
100–102; and 100 percent
valuations, 80–81, 83; open
space plan for, 79, 82–89,
106–7; purchase of un-
developed land in, 57–62; and

relocation of Route 2, 79–80; report on undeveloped land in, 88–91; and Rural Land Foundation, 62–64; survey of remaining undeveloped land in, 78–79; two-acre zoning in, 68, 71; and Umbrello property, 102–6; wetland mapping and zoning in, 76–78. *See also* Conservation Commission; Farrah Pond Village; Planning Board; Rural Land Foundation

Lincoln Institute of Land Policy, 49

Lincoln Land Conservation Trust, 57, 63, 64, 147

Lincoln Mall, 76

Lincoln Ridge, 98, 107, 150

Lincoln Woods, 73, 74–75, 122, 150

Little, Charles E., 18

McCall, Tom, 51

McHarg, Ian, 134

Maine, University of, 119

Maine Association of Conservation Commissions, 119

Maine Coast Heritage Trust, 119

Marcin, Thomas C., 29–30

Martha's Vineyard, preservation of bulk of Katama Farm on, 128–30

Mason, Max, 63

Massachusetts, University of, 69, 123; College of Food and Agriculture of, 137

Massachusetts Agricultural Lands Preservation Committee, 35, 137

Massachusetts Association of Conservation Commissions, 136

Massachusetts Audubon Society, 27, 56, 79, 136; "Comparative Economics of Conservation versus Development" published by, 118; "Shape Your Land Use Destiny" published by, 113–17

Massachusetts Department of Natural Resources, 65, 118

Massachusetts Institute of Technology (MIT), 136

Massachusetts Land League, 136

Massachusetts Self-Help Fund, 66

Mayer, Jean, 22, 138

Maynard, Massachusetts, open space plan prepared for, 130–31

Metropolitan District Commission (MDC, Boston), 35, 36, 78, 95, 139–40

Minuteman National Park (Concord-Lincoln-Lexington), 79–80, 100, 110

Morill Act (1862), 138

Morine, David, 55

Mt. Misery acquisition, 65–68

Moynihan, Daniel Patrick, 25

National Agricultural Land Policy Act, 46

National Geodetic Survey maps, 145

National Trust for Historic Preservation, 27

Natural resources: protection of, 9; steps to follow for protection of, 145–47; USDA publication on current and prospective supplies and uses of, 13–15. *See also* Land; Land use; Water resources

Nature Conservancy, The, 27, 55, 110, 142

Nearing, Helen and Scott, *Living the Good Life,* 26

Neighborhood Lot Program, 88, 102

New Alchemy, The, 27

Newton, Massachusetts, undeveloped land in, 131–33

Newton Conservators, 131

Northeast Association of Agricultural Secretaries, 138

Northeast Association of State Departments of Agriculture, 43

Northfield, Massachusetts, 140

Norumbega, 36

Olmstead, Frederic Law, 78

100 percent valuations, Lincoln's, 80–81, 83

1000 Friends of Oregon, 50, 52

Open space plans (Massachusetts): Ipswich, 133–34; Lincoln, 79, 82–89, 106–7; Maynard, 130–31

Open Space Residential District (OSRD), 71, 73, 92, 98

Oregon Land Conservation and Development Commission (LCDC), 52

Paine, Tom: "Common Sense," 142–43; "Crisis Papers," 143

Pennsylvania, University of, 69

Petrillo, Joseph, 49

Philadelphia, *see* Delaware Valley Region, including Philadelphia

Pierce, John, 63

Planning Board (Lincoln, Massachusetts), 65, 68, 85; and cluster development, 99; and Lincoln Mall, 76; Neighborhood Lot Program of, 88, 102; and wetland zoning, 77; and Winchell property, 70–71

Pollution, effects of air, on crop yields, 18

Population growth: land use and, 2–4, 24; projections of future, 24–25, 29, 147–48

Portland, Maine, growth and land use conflicts in, 37–40
Portland, Oregon, growth and land use conflicts in, 49–52
Precipitation, distribution of, 19
Property taxes, 119–20
Proposition 13, California's, 119
Public Law 92–500, 21

Reilly, William K., 50
Revere, Paul, 55
Rhode Island School of Design (RISD), 141, 143
Richmond, Henry R., 50, 52
Riparian Doctrine, 21
Rookery Bay (Florida), land use practices threatening, 128
Route 2, relocation of, 79–80
Rural Land Foundation (Lincoln, Massachusetts), 57–58, 90, 147; and Codman property, 70–76 passim; and Lincoln Mall, 76; organization of, 62; purchase of Wheeler Farm by, 62–63, 64; and Umbrello property, 103–4, 105–6

Sandy Pond Trust, 100–102
San Francisco, California, growth and land use conflicts in, 47–49
Sanibel/Captiva Conservation Foundation, 134
Sanibel, Florida, land use plan for, 134–35

Schuylkill Valley Nature Center, 42
"Set-aside" programs, 15
"Shape Your Land Use Destiny" (Robert A. Lemire), 113–17, 119
Sierra Club, The, 27
Slash and burn operations, 13
Society for the Preservation of Cape Cod, 121
Society for the Preservation of New England Antiquities, 64
Soil Conservation Service, see under U.S. Department of Agriculture
State Street Bank and Trust Company, 62

Thoreau, Henry David, 67, 100
Todd, John, 27
Trust for Public Land (TPL), 27, 49, 127
Tufts Environmental Center, 136

Umbrello property, 102–6
"Undeveloped Land in Lincoln, Massachusetts" (report), 88–91
University of Massachusetts Technical Guidance Center Bulletin, 119
U.S. Census Bureau, 25

U.S. Department of Agriculture (USDA), 6, 150; draft policy statement of Land Use Executive Committee of, 16–17; Economic Research Service of, 24; Forest Service of, 29; "Our Land and Water Resources, Current and Prospective Supplies and Uses," 13–15; Soil Conservation Service of, 50, 69, 76; soil conservation study of cropland availability of, 15–16

Vineyard Conservation Society, 129, 130
Vineyard Open Land Foundation, 129–30

Walden Pond (Lincoln, Massachusetts), 65, 67, 100, 110–11
Wallace, McHarg, Robert & Todd, 134

Water resources: Boston area's, 35–37; problems with, 139–40; protection of, 28; state of, 19–22
Wetlands, saving of, through mapping and zoning, 10, 76–78
Wheeler Farm (Lincoln, Massachusetts), 61–62, 63, 64
Winchell property, 68, 70, 71–72, 92, 95
Worldwatch Institute, 17
Wunderlich, Gene, 24

Zoning, 10; absence of planning and, 23; compensatory versus noncompensatory, 51, 148–49; and mapping, Lincoln's wetland, 10, 76–78
Zoning Board of Appeals (Lincoln, Massachusetts), 71, 77